Françoise Hardy

By the same author

By Swords Divided: Corfe Castle in the Civil War. Halsgrove, 2003.
Thomas Hardy: Christmas Carollings. Halsgrove, 2005.
Enid Blyton and her Enchantment with Dorset. Halsgrove, 2005.
Tyneham: A Tribute. Halsgrove, 2007.
Agatha Christie: The Finished Portrait. Tempus, 2007.
The Story of George Loveless and the Tolpuddle Martyrs. Halsgrove, 2008.
Father of the Blind: A Portrait of Sir Arthur Pearson. The History Press, 2009.
Agatha Christie: The Pitkin Guide. Pitkin Publishing, 2009.
Arthur Conan Doyle: The Man behind Sherlock Holmes. The History Press, 2009.
HMS Hood: Pride of the Royal Navy. The History Press, 2009.
Purbeck Personalities. Halsgrove, 2009.
Bournemouth's Founders and Famous Visitors. The History Press, 2010.
Thomas Hardy: Behind the Mask. The History Press, 2011.
Hitler: Dictator or Puppet. Pen & Sword Books, 2011.
A Brummie Boy goes to War. Halsgrove, 2011.
Winston Churchill: Portrait of an Unquiet Mind. Pen & Sword Books, 2012.
Charles Darwin: Destroyer of Myths. Pen & Sword Books, 2013.
Beatrix Potter: Her Inner World. Pen & Sword Books, 2013.
T.E. Lawrence: Tormented Hero. Fonthill, 2014.
Agatha Christie: The Disappearing Novelist. Fonthill, 2014.
Lawrence of Arabia's Clouds Hill. Halsgrove, 2014.
Jane Austen: Love is Like a Rose. Fonthill, 2015.
Kindly Light: The Story of Blind Veterans UK. Fonthill, 2015.
Thomas Hardy at Max Gate: The Latter Years. Halsgrove, 2016.
Corfe Remembered. Halsgrove, 2017.
Thomas Hardy: Bockhampton and Beyond. Halsgrove, 2017.
Mugabe: Monarch of Blood and Tears. Austin Macauley, 2017

Making Sense of Marilyn. Fonthill, 2018.
Hitler's Insanity: A Conspiracy of Silence. Fonthill, 2018.
The Unwitting Fundamentalist. Austin Macauley, 2018.
Robert Mugabe's Lost Jewel of Africa. Fonthill, 2018.
Bound for the East Indies: Halsewell – A Shipwreck that Gripped the Nation, Fonthill, 2020.
Beatrix Potter: Her Inner World, Pen & Sword Books, 2020.
The Real Peter Sellers. White Owl 2021
Paul Robeson. New Haven Publishing 2022

Author's website: https://www.andrew-norman.co.uk
Amazon Author Profile: amazon.co.uk: 'Andrew Norman: Books, Biography, Blogs'

Françoise Hardy

A musical tale of love and loss

Andrew Norman

NEW HAVEN PUBLISHING

Published 2022
First Edition
NEW HAVEN PUBLISHING LTD
www.newhavenpublishingltd.com
newhavenpublishing@gmail.com

All Rights Reserved
The rights of Andrew Norman, as the author of this work, have been asserted in accordance with the Copyrights, Designs and Patents Act 1988.
No part of this book may be re-printed or reproduced or utilized in any form or by any electronic, mechanical or other means, now unknown or hereafter invented, including photocopying, and recording, or in any information storage or retrieval system, without the written permission of the
Author and Publisher.

Front cover © Brooks, Charlotte, and Thomas R Koeniges, photographer. *Image from LOOK - Job 66- titled Françoise Hardy.* Dec. 7 date added to Look's library. Photograph. Retrieved from the Library of Congress, <www.loc.gov/item/2021685561/>.
Back Cover © Brooks, Charlotte, and Thomas R Koeniges, photographer. *Image from LOOK - Job 66- titled Françoise Hardy.* Dec. 7 date added to Look's library. Photograph. Retrieved from the Library of Congress, <www.loc.gov/item/2021685558/>.

Cover Design © Pete Cunliffe

Copyright © 2022 Andrew Norman
All rights reserved
ISBN: 978-1-912587-67-4

Contents

Introduction	9
1 Françoise Hardy (born 17 January 1944)	11
2 Françoise and Her Family	13
3 Françoise: Feelings of Shame and Inferiority	18
4 John Bowlby: Child Care and the Growth of Love	21
5 1966: A Youthful and Seemingly Happy Françoise	24
6 Music Beckons!	27
7 The Road to Success!	32
8 1960: Romance with Jean-Marie Périer and Further Success	37
9 About Jacques Dutronc	41
10 1966: Françoise Hardy and Jacques Dutronc	43
11 Further Success	46
12 Literature: Some Favourite Authors	48
13 A Young, Joyful, and Vivacious Françoise	50
14 1971: An Interview with Jacques Dutronc	52
15 Getting to Know Jacques Better: Peter McEnery	54
16 September 1967: Françoise and Jacques – A Serious Relationship Commences	60
17 Françoise and Jacques: Meltdown!	62
18 A New Arrival: Thomas Dutronc, 16 June 1973	68
19 Meanwhile, Life Goes On	75
20 The Wedding: 30 March 1981	78
21 With Her Music, Triumph!	81

22 With Jacques, Disaster! Spiritualism: Health Problems Loom	83
23 What Françoise Longed For and what was On Offer	90
24 Françoise and Jacques: An Avoidant Relationship	92
25 'Commitment Avoidancy' and its Origins	96
26 What If?	101
27 Françoise's Incredible Perseverance!	102
28 How Easy it is to Fall in Love with the Wrong Person!	105
29 Jacques Expresses Remorse	107
30 Françoise's Coping Mechanisms: How She Made Sense of the Long Separations that were Imposed Upon Her	108
31 Françoise Loses Patience: Letting go of the Dream and Summoning the Strength to Walk Away	111
32 Françoise Reveals Herself through her Own Lyrics	113
33 Living Alone: Solitude	126
34 A 'Thank You' to Jacques!	128
35 Some Help and Guidance for the Avoider	129
36 Some of Françoise's Other Admirers	131
37 The Camera Never Lies!	134
38 Sylvie Duval	140
39 The Significance of Eye Contact	141
40 'Falling for Françoise'	144
41 Illness	147
42 Faith; Mortality; The Afterlife	148
Epilogue	150

Introduction

In the early 1960s a new 'star' appeared on the pop music scene and burned brightly in the firmament. This was the enchantingly beautiful and charming French singer-songwriter ('chanteuse-compositrice'), Françoise Hardy.

My first introduction to anything French was in the 1950s, when my family left England for Central Africa and lived in Southern Rhodesia (now Zimbabwe) for a period of three years. Here, at school under the heat of the African sun, my fellow pupils and I were taught French. Some of us also attended extra French lessons on Tuesday afternoons, our teacher being the youthful Miss Boyer. What attracted me to 'extra French' was the enthusiasm of our teacher, and the romance of that beautiful language. Very soon, phrases such as 'J'ai perdu la plume de ma tante' ('I have lost my aunt's quill'), and 'À quelle heure arrivons-nous à St Benoît?' (What time do we arrive at St Benoît?') tripped off our tongues.

As an undergraduate, and subsequently a medical student at Oxford, long before marriage, children and camping holidays in the French Alps and Pyrenees, I was aware of the singer Françoise Hardy and of her beautiful songs, the lyrics and music of which were often of her own composition.

When a back injury cut short my medical career and I became a writer of biographies, I decided to include Françoise in my repertoire. This was not only on account of her magnificent contribution to the music of the day, but also because there were certain aspects of her character and behaviour which I found to be enigmatic, and therefore worth exploring.

Unlike with many of the popular musicians of the time, with Françoise there was no blaring music or wild gesticulations. She had no need of devices such as these. I found her songs captivating, and still do, particularly those about love, loneliness, and loss.

During the early years, sometimes a flicker of a smile played about her lips but otherwise, I noticed how serious she looked. This must be due to nervousness – 'stage fright', I thought. But to my surprise, even when she had become famous, there was still a look of pathos about her. This was the case even when she was being interviewed. There was very little laughter, and instead, she would sit on the edge of her chair, wide-eyed and in a defensive position, with arms folded. But always, I observed, she looked her interviewer straight in the eye, which to my mind was a sign of absolute honesty, even if at times she was bemused by the banality of the questions, for Françoise is a highly intelligent woman.

Why did Françoise never 'lighten up', at least, not until her later years? Was it conceivable that this French icon, beloved by millions of all nationalities throughout the world and who, evidently, had the world at her feet, was permanently troubled?

In fact, yes, there was something disturbing Françoise, and that something was not simply a legacy of the troublesome childhood that she had experienced, for it continued for most if not all of her adult life. Many people have described the calming effect of hearing Françoise sing, and yet it is doubtful whether her millions of adoring fans outside of France had the slightest notion that her private life was in a state of perpetual turmoil.

1
Françoise Hardy (born 17 January 1944)

Françoise Madeleine Hardy was born in Nazi-occupied Paris, France, on 17 January 1944, at the Marie-Louise Clinic, avenue des Martyrs in the 9th arrondissement (administrative district), France having been invaded by Germany on 10 May 1940.[1]

Françoise's mother was Madeleine Jeanne Hardy, born in 1920, and her home address was 24 rue d'Aumale. Their apartment, said Françoise, was tiny. Her father was Pierre Marie Étienne Dillard, who was two decades Madeleine's senior. Pierre was a married man, wealthy, and who owned a stationer's shop in the city.

'I was born at nine thirty in the evening during an air raid alert', said Françoise.[2] This was the 5th year of the war, and on 6 June 1944, when Françoise was only 4 months old, the Allies invaded northern France, prior to liberating that country from the scourge of Hitler's Nazis. Meanwhile, the Allies were currently bombing French railways and other strategic targets.

On 23 July 1945, Françoise's sister Michèle, who was also the offspring of an affair between Madeleine and Pierre, was born. Françoise, however, admitted to having 'a confused desire to have [her] mother for [herself] alone'.[3]

The 9th arrondissement contained many places of cultural, historic, and architectural interest. For example, the Palais Garnier, home to the Paris Opera (the principal opera and ballet company of France); the Boulevard Haussmann, with its department stores including Les Galeries Lafayette and Le Printemps; and the Folies Bergère theatre.

1. Hardy, Françoise, *The Despair of Monkeys and Other Trifles*, p.1.

2. Ibid, p.1.
3. Ibid, p.5.

2
Françoise and Her Family

In her book *The Despair of Monkeys and Other Trifles*, Françoise revealed a great deal about her immediate family, and of the dynamics within that family.[1]

When Françoise was born, her mother Madeleine was aged 23. Françoise described Madeleine as being a woman of 'exceptional beauty' who, at five foot eight inches, was tall for a woman in those days.[2]

A measure of her mother's love was that when she took the infant Françoise to Paris's square de la Trinité 'for some fresh air', they were caught up in a gun battle and Madeleine 'threw herself over [her] carriage to protect [her] from the bullets'.[3] This, of course, was when the Second World War was raging.

Madeleine, said Françoise, was not 'truly in love' with her father Pierre. He was 'madly in love' with her, but she 'merely felt flattered that a man of his standing would be interested in her'.[4] Furthermore, whereas Pierre had received an education and enjoyed 'a much higher social status',[5] her mother Madeleine was from a humble and provincial background, her parents being 'low level bank employees who only read the newspapers and had a poor command of the French language'. 'As soon as she got her diploma [in bookkeeping]', said Françoise, Madeleine left home 'to find work in the capital'.[6]

As far as her father's relationship with her mother was concerned, said Françoise, discretion was vital. 'It was essential that no one in his circle knew, if not of our very existence [i.e. that of herself and her sister], at least of the family bond between us.'[7] Such subterfuge was hardly likely to instil confidence in Françoise and her sister Michèle.

Michèle was born at a time when Madeleine was working as a bookkeeper's assistant and barely making ends meet. Such financial constraints obliged Madeleine to send Michèle to her maternal grandparents, Claudius Hardy and Louise Jeanne Milot (known as Jeanne), who brought her up.[8]

'I loved my mother passionately and exclusively', said Françoise, 'as I had no one but her to love and I was the first person for whom she had ever felt deeply'.[9] In fact, she described her relationship with her mother as an 'addiction' on her part.[10] Madeleine had a 'strong constitution', said Françoise, but 'the fear of losing her tormented me throughout my childhood'.[11]

Françoise confessed to idealizing her father Pierre 'more than he deserved, considering [they] barely saw him; he was content with only having lunch with [them] in Aulnay during the Christmas, Easter, and Pentecost holidays'. This was a reference to 5 rue du Tilleul, Aulnay-sous-Bois, a town in the north-eastern suburbs of Paris, the home of Françoise's maternal grandparents Claudius and Jeanne. Her father Pierre 'sweetly called [her] "Patchouli"', she said.[12] This is an aromatic oil obtained from a south-east Asian shrub which is used in perfumery, which was very popular in France in the 1960s and 1970s, initially amongst hippies but also teenagers and youngsters of the day. It was reputed to disguise the smell of marijuana.

'My sister and I spent our childhood and adolescence in a vacuum that consisted of the house at Aulnay and the small apartment in the 9th arrondissement where no visitors ever came', said Françoise. This was with one exception: Jean Isorni, 'a rejected suitor' of her mother's.

However, in the 1950s, there were frequent visits from Gilbert von Giannellia, an Austrian Baron who 'was probably the only man with whom my mother had ever fallen in love'. But the Baron attempted to borrow money from Madeleine, 'when she did not have a penny to spare'.[13]

Françoise had no love for her maternal grandmother Jeanne, whom she described as 'despicable'. As for her maternal grandfather Claudius, he 'seemed to ignore his grandchildren'.[14] He 'only spoke to me once, in 1962', she said, to ask 'are you happy, at least?'[15]

When Françoise was sent to her grandparents, she said, this 'plunged me back into a hostile world far from the only person I loved and who loved me'.[16] This, of course, was a reference to her mother Madeleine. At Aulnay, where the sisters were obliged to spend their vacations, life was 'strictly regulated'. Françoise and Michèle were required by their grandmother to make their beds, dust the furniture, prepare the vegetables, do the washing up, etc.[17] Discipline was rigorously enforced. For example, if Françoise and Michèle did not finish their main meal, they 'would have to go without dessert'.[18] Also, attendance at mass on Sundays, and saying their prayers before going to bed, were mandatory.[19] A frustration for Françoise was that most of her grandparents' books were 'locked away in the library'.[20] How did Françoise react to this discipline? 'I was docile and timid', she said.[21]

Their mother Madeleine stayed at Aulnay at weekends, but when she returned to Paris where she worked, the time, for Françoise, 'seemed to drag on endlessly because all I cared about was my mother's return'. She found, however, that the 'crushing feeling of loneliness', would 'fly away whenever [she] managed to isolate [herself] in a book. This practically sums up [her] whole life: a life lived by proxy, more virtual than real'.[22] Again, this peripatetic lifestyle was one hardly calculated to make Françoise feel secure.

There were enjoyable interludes, however; visits to Paris, to the department stores and 'the floor with the toys' or to the place where the perfumes and cosmetics, with their 'intoxicating fragrances' were displayed.[23] And 'when the nice weather came, [they] would walk to the Jardin des Tuileries, with quasi-ritual stops along the way in front of the pastry shops where, for want of anything better, [they] would devour the cakes with [their] eyes'.[24]

Françoise also loved her grandparents' garden, where rose bushes 'climbed along the stone walls and smelled so good, just like the privet flowers looking out onto the street'. The theme of 'flowers' would one day feature strongly in the songs that Françoise composed. She also enjoyed the wonderful apricot preserves, gooseberry jelly and apple tarts that her aunt made. Six decades later, Françoise would say, 'Even today, baking brings me indescribable pleasure'.[25]

At home in the rue d'Aumale, said Françoise, the 'school schedule was strict', but her mother was even stricter, and she and her sister would be woken up each morning at 6.00 a.m. and sent to bed each evening at 7.30 p.m.[26]

Madeleine was clearly devoted to her two daughters, and she 'would bleed herself dry every year' to give them a 'dream Christmas', with Christmas tree, and one present each, of their choice, as that was all she could afford.

From this account, it is clear that Françoise had an overwhelming desire to be loved and cherished. However, the circumstances of her birth and upbringing, and in particular her fraught relationship with her maternal grandmother Jeanne, were hardly conducive to confidence building, and instead acted to make her feel inferior.

Later in life, Françoise described how these childhood experiences had left her with a legacy of shyness. The reason for this shyness, she said, was as follows. 'I was aware that my family situation was not normal. In the first place, I thought my parents were divorced, and at that time it [i.e. divorce] was not a good thing, you know. It was a kind of shame. And, at the same time, my father didn't help much financially my mother, and all the other little girls were dressed in a very different way than I was. Their parents had more money than my poor mother, who was working hard all the time but who didn't have money at all.'[27]

1. Hardy, Françoise, *The Despair of Monkeys and Other Trifles*, p.1.
2. Ibid, p.1.
3. Ibid, p.9.
4. Ibid, p.2.
5. Ibid, p.1.
6. Ibid, p.2.
7. Ibid, p.11.
8. Ibid, p.4.
9. Ibid, p.5.
10. Ibid, p.10.
11. Ibid, p.10.

12. Ibid, p.5.
13. Ibid, pp.4-5.
14. Ibid, p.5.
15. Ibid, p.3.
16. Ibid, p.11.
17. Ibid, p.7.
18. Ibid, p.7.
19. Ibid, p.7.
20. Ibid, p.9.
21. Ibid, p.20.
22. Ibid, p.7.
23. Ibid, p.6.
24. Ibid, p.6.
25. Ibid, p.8.
26. Ibid, p.9.
27. Hardy, Françoise, interview with John Andrew, BBC Radio 4, 2011.

3
Françoise: Feelings of Shame and Inferiority

It was their father Pierre's wish that his daughters should attend a religious school so, said Françoise, 'our entire schooling was with the Trinitarian [Order of the Catholic Church] sisters who taught at 42 rue Bruyère, a five-minute walk from where we lived'. However, added Françoise, 'I detested school' and 'this is where the feeling of shame that has tormented me non-stop since I was a child took root'.

There were several reasons for this. As already mentioned, Françoise believed (mistakenly) that her parents were a divorced couple, which 'at this time and in this kind of place was still viewed as deplorable'. Her father was invariably late when it came to paying the school fees. Also, as a pupil with above average intelligence, she was made to 'skip two grades' which would have meant that her classmates were a year older than she was. Because her mother was poor, she was obliged to wear 'bargain-basement skirts' until they were 'threadbare'. But 'Most importantly, there was the awkwardness', on Françoise's part, 'of an introvert who did not share other people's interests and was never able to fit in'.

In order to avoid having to play sports, Françoise used to hide in the chapel. This was misinterpreted by the 'good sisters', who saw this 'sensible, hardworking, and solitary young girl, who preferred praying to playing' as 'showing signs of an early religious vocation'. Whereupon she became the teachers' 'pet' which served to 'widen the gap between [her] and the others even more'.[1]

Françoise's maternal grandmother Jeanne added greatly to her low self-esteem: she made 'so many scornful observations about my physical appearance that I grew up convinced that I was more ugly than average'. The trauma of this would be a lasting legacy

'I have never managed to completely rid myself of the neurosis this gave me' she said.[2]

Finally, Françoise tolerated her 'ordeal' of school in order, she said, 'that my mother would be pleased with me'.[3]

Years later, Françoise described how, suddenly, she was transported into paradise. The Baron von Giannellia persuaded her mother to send her daughters to an Austrian family, the Weslers, in order to learn German. Here, she and Michèle spent successive summers in the 1950s. This involved a train journey on the Orient Express (luxury long-distance passenger train), from Paris's Gare de l'Est. As 'the train began to move' and Madeleine's 'long silhouette gradually disappeared, my despair touched rock bottom and I would have given anything to stay in Paris with her', said Françoise.[4]

Nonetheless, Françoise had happy times with Hedwig Wesler – 'Aunt Heidi' -, a widow whose husband and eldest son had been killed in the war. There were cycle rides through the forest with Hedwig's son Gunni and daughter Gertrud; and there was swimming in the lake; 'fresh, foamy milk' to be had from the farm, and hide-and-seek in the farmer's barn.

Subsequently, long after the death of 'Aunt Heidi' Françoise would 'put back the clock', to a time when 'a lifetime of love would still be stretching out' before them all. She recalled: I would 'concentrate on her [Heidi] so strongly that I would eventually see her again on the doorstep, hastily drying her flour-covered hands in her apron; her opal eyes would brighten when she saw me. Barely recovered from her surprise, she would spread out her arms while joyfully shouting: "Franziska!" and I would run to her calling back "Aunt Heidi, Aunt Heidi!"'.[5]

Throughout these times, Françoise had shown both resilience and an unconditional loyalty to her mother Madeleine. She had also demonstrated her ability to be happy in the company of those whom she loved.

1. Hardy, Françoise, *The Despair of Monkeys and Other Trifles*, pp.12-13.
2. Ibid, p.20.

3. Ibid, p.13.
4. Ibid, p.15.
5. Ibid, pp.18-19.

4
John Bowlby: Child Care and the Growth of Love

In 1965, in what would become one of the undisputed milestones in the study of child psychology, *Child Care and the Growth of Love* by British psychiatrist and psychoanalyst John Bowlby was published.

Bowlby stated as follows: 'Among the most significant developments of psychiatry during the past quarter of a century has been the steady growth of evidence that the quality of the paternal care which a child receives in his [or, in the context of this narrative, 'her' – i.e. Françoise's] earliest years is of vital importance for his future mental health.'[1]

It was, said Bowlby, 'this complex, rich, and rewarding relationship with the mother in early years, varied in countless ways by relations with the father, and with the brothers and sisters, that child psychiatrists and many others now believe underlie the development of character and of mental health'.[2] Sadly, Françoise was never able to form an emotional bond with her only sibling, her sister Michèle.

A cause of maternal deprivation, 'in which parent-child relationships may become unhealthy', said Bowlby, was 'an unconsciously rejecting attitude underlying a loving one'.[3] This was certainly the case with Claudius and Jeanne, Françoise's maternal grandparents, with whom she spent the summer vacations.

Bowlby described a child's relationship with his mother as being 'by far his most important relationship during these years. It is she who feeds and cleans him, keeps him warm, and comforts him. It is to his mother that he turns when in distress. In the young child's eyes, the father plays second fiddle, and his value increases only as the child becomes more able to stand alone'.[4]

Unfortunately, although Françoise 'idealized' her father Pierre, he was hardly ever present in her life.

The father was also of value in respect of his 'economic and emotional support of the mother', continued Bowlby.[5] To what extent this was the case in respect of Pierre and Madeleine is not known for certain.

Maternal deprivation could also be the result of a child being separated from its parents. Bowlby spoke of 'the absolute need of infants and toddlers for the continuous care of their mothers'. In response to the question put by the mother, 'Can I then never leave my child?', the answer was yes.[6] But 'Naturally a mother will keep the time she is away from the child as short as possible, though in some cases the length of time lies outside her control. The holiday whilst granny looks after the baby, which so many mothers and fathers of young children pine for, is best kept to a week or ten days'. In Madeleine's case, it was not a matter of going on holiday. She was the breadwinner, and her poverty obliged her to go out to work!

However, 'After the child has reached about three years, rather longer holidays from children can be taken safely, provided always that the child is in the care of someone he likes and trusts, and that the anxieties which will inevitably be aroused in him are recognised and respected'.[7] Françoise certainly disliked her grandmother Jeanne, and for good reason. As for her grandfather Claudius, he appeared largely to ignore her. The summer vacations spent with them were far too long for Françoise's liking, and this caused her a great deal of anguish.

Finally, said Bowlby, 'it is by no means clear why some children are damaged' by maternal deprivation, 'and some are not'.[8]

When a child does not have a loving, caring and stable relationship with his or her mother, said Bowlby, a state of 'maternal deprivation' is said to exist: 'The ill-effects of deprivation vary with its degree. Partial deprivation brings in its train anxiety, excessive need for love, powerful feelings of revenge, and, arising from these last, guilt and depression. A young child, still immature in mind and body, cannot cope with all these emotions and drives. The way in which he responds to these disturbances of his inner life may in the end bring about nervous disorders and instability of character.'[9]

Françoise certainly experienced maternal deprivation, which was no fault of her mother but due to circumstances. As for her father, he was absent for most of the time. The question is, would this leave a lasting and negative legacy on her as an adult?

1. Bowlby, John, *Child Care and the Growth of Love*, p.13.
2. Ibid, p.13.
3. Ibid, p.15.
4. Ibid, p.15.
5. Ibid, p.15.
6. Ibid, p.18.
7. Ibid, p.19.
8. Ibid, p.22.
9. Ibid, p.14.

5
1966: A Youthful and Seemingly Happy Françoise

In an interview that she gave to Belgian television in 1966, when she was 22, Françoise was visible on camera, but the interviewer, Stéphane Steenman was not.

Throughout the interview, Françoise sat attentively, looking as demure as ever, and clearly wondering what was in store for her. With her steadfast gaze fixed on the interviewer throughout, she was the epitome of honesty and integrity.

A series of questions was fired at her. They alternated in subject matter between interesting aspects of her career and inane references to her personal habits and preferences. Their aim was seemingly to destabilise her and see how well she fared under pressure. Nonetheless, she kept her composure, parrying the questions deftly, with a quizzical expression on her face. Still, the look of incredulity at the banality and triviality of the questions betrayed her emotions. And as they arrived in rapid succession she was, at one point, lost for words, eventually bursting out laughing at the silliness of the entire process. Years later, Françoise declared: 'Over the course of my forty-six years of professional activity, two thirds of the journalists I have dealt with have asked me insipid questions and then twisted my answers, thereby misrepresenting - consciously or not - my intentions.'[1]

Grand Prix was a US sports drama film directed by John Frankenheimer (released 21 December 1966) in which Françoise played the part of 'Lisa'. In regard to the movie, Françoise was asked 'Why did you accept a role so transparent?'. The answer was delivered with a smile: 'Because it was very well paid!' 'Why haven't you changed your hairstyle when you've changed the style of your songs?' 'I don't think I have changed the style of my songs.', she answered. 'Why, my dear Françoise, aren't you at the head of a fashion house?' At being patronised in this way by someone who was ignorant, Françoise did not bat an eyelid. She simply smiled and answered demurely: 'Because I'm not a businesswoman'. Then came the question 'If, tomorrow, the fashion was for very long skirts, would you wear very long skirts immediately?' She replied 'I think fashion, at least winter fashion, is already for very long skirts.' Once again, the interviewer had betrayed his ignorance. 'I wear what suits me', she continued, 'whether long or short. If a fashion suits me, I wear it.'

Suddenly, out of the blue, came the question, 'Why don't you get married, Françoise?' She stared at the interviewer in astonishment, at this highly personal intrusion, asked without any preamble whatsoever. Again, not only did she keep her composure, she chuckled at the thought of it, and a wonderful smile lit up her face. 'Because I've not found my soulmate, and mainly because I don't want a child now. And I believe the only reason for getting married is if you want to have a child.' One day, Françoise would indeed encounter a person who she regarded as a soulmate, but would he regard her likewise?

Meanwhile, when asked if she would accept the role of an actress, for example in the part of Chimène at La Comédie Française (French National Theatre, Paris), she replied with characteristic modesty: 'No, I'm not talented at all for acting.'

Now came another intrusion, and again a patronising one. 'Françoise, how many records have you sold, my dear?' This was meant with a look of muted astonishment. 'I really don't know.' The interviewer now returned to a topic about which he appeared to be obsessed. 'Would you accept to cut your hair for a leading role?' 'I don't know. Maybe. It depends.' Finally, Françoise was asked who was her least favourite singer? 'My least favourite? I know that my favourite singer is Barbara' [this was the stage name of French singer Monique Andrée Serf]. But I have no idea who my least favourite is' she replied diplomatically.[2]

What can be deduced about Françoise from this interview? That she had displayed a maturity beyond her years, had retained her composure and her dignity when 'under fire', had recognised the humour in the situation, and most importantly of all, had not been afraid to express her own opinions. This was indeed a creditable performance on her part, if a somewhat cringeworthy one on the part of the interviewer.

Finally, whatever the deprivations and hardships of her childhood, as yet this appeared to have had no adverse effect on Françoise, outwardly at least.

1. Hardy, Françoise, *The Despair of Monkeys and Other Trifles*, p.212
2. Hardy, Françoise: Interview 1966, YouTube.

6
Music Beckons!

As a child, Françoise dreamed of becoming a trapeze artist, but having no trapeze to practice on, she said, 'I devoted my free time to practicing acrobatic routines with my sister'.[1]

Once a year, said Françoise, after Christmas lunch, she and her family went to the cinema. On one occasion, she saw a film of *Romeo and Juliet*, performed by the Ballets Russes, an itinerant ballet company based in Paris. It was based on William Shakespeare's eponymous tragedy, about the doomed romance of two teenage lovers. 'This movie was a revelation that dazzled me as much as it tore me apart'. That was on account of its beauty. Having received some dancing slippers for Christmas when she was aged 12, Françoise began dancing lessons 'in a studio next to the Champs-Élysées Theatre'. However, the physical strain of the lessons proved to be too much.[2]

As a teenager, said Françoise, the radio was of great importance in her life. She heard the songs that she had 'set [her] heart on expressed', she said, and she purchased sheet music in order to learn them herself.[3] Before long she was well and truly 'hooked'! 'I have never really taken any drugs', said Françoise, 'but I have always compared it to music. You end up unable to live without a particular melody and then, when its effect has waned, you spend your time looking for another one which has the same impact'.[4]

Towards the end of the 1950s, when Françoise was in her mid-teens, she 'discovered a station that played non-stop English and American country rock performed by very young artists. [She] immediately identified with them because they expressed teenage loneliness and awkwardness over melodies that were much more inspiring than their texts'.[5] This was the British privately-owned radio station Radio Luxembourg, 'your station of the stars' (this was the station's catchphrase!), she once said laughingly during an interview. 'At that time you could hear Elvis Presley, Cliff Richard, Connie Francis, Brenda Lee, people like that, Marty Wilde". "These were your early influences then, really?" "Yes" she replied.[6]

In other words:

- Pop (Popular) music: originated in Britain in the mid-1950s, as a description for rock and roll and then the new youth music styles that it influenced.[7]

Paul Anka was her favourite performer, surpassing in her mind even Georges Guétary [French singer, dancer, cabaret performer, and film actor].[8]

Françoise mentioned on song in particular, "So Sad" by The Everly Brothers, as having had an influence on her:

> We used to have good times together
> But now I feel them slip away
> It makes me cry to see love die
> So sad to watch good love go bad.

- Rock and roll: a type of popular dance music originating in the 1950s, characterised by a heavy, strong beat and simple melodies.[9]

Her father Pierre played the piano, said Françoise, and she herself received piano lessons when 'still very young'. This was not to her liking. However, when her mother's friend the Baron von Giannellia arrived on the scene, 'he gave [her] mother a turntable and two classical music records'. One was of Beethoven's 7th Symphony, of which Françoise declared, 'I used to listen to this music while reading fairy tales and feeling strange and happy. When music is beautiful, it can take you to a mysterious dimension, even when you are 5 years old'.[10]

'My daily discovery of melodies on the radio, each more exhilarating than the last, turned my life upside down', said Françoise, who 'fell under the spell' of Georges Guétary.[11]

With the money that she had been paid for giving German lessons to a 14-year-old boy, Françoise rushed to a record shop on Paris's rue de la Chaussée-d'Antin. But disappointingly, the proprietor had not heard of the records that she wished to purchase: by Eddie Cochran, the Everly Brothers, Brenda Lee, Neil Sedaka, Cliff Richard, and Billy Fury.[12] At that time, she said, 'In secret I was nurturing the ambition of finding an activity with some connection to the musical style I had recently fallen for'.[13]

At the age of 16, Françoise passed her baccalaureate examinations, (French national academic qualification that pupils obtain on completion of secondary education), whereupon, at her mother's urging, her father purchased a guitar for her. Having received her guitar, said Françoise, 'I had a small method to learn some chords, so that I knew three or four chords. And I found out very quickly that I could find a tune which was more or less like all the tunes I was listening to on Radio Luxembourg'. She laughed. 'At that time, I was composing maybe one song a day.' And then, with characteristic modesty, 'They were all very bad! They were all terrible!'[14]

Françoise's mother Madeleine, however, had other ideas and 'marched [her] off to enrol in the Institut d'Études Politiques', an institute for the study of political science. This was in autumn 1960, when Françoise was aged only 'sixteen and a half'. The exercise was not a success.[15]

However, it was while she was studying at the Institut d'Études Politiques, said Françoise, that she experienced sexual intercourse for the first time. 'Convinced my future would be that of a nun and flattered by the attention I was receiving from a boy for the first time, I thought I was in love', she said. However, during what she euphemistically described as 'the operation', she 'felt nothing' and was 'relieved' that it was over, and that she 'had taken the first step towards normality'.[16]

In spring 1961, Françoise commenced as an undergraduate at Paris's Sorbonne University, to study German. And in her spare time, she 'wrote three or four songs a week'.[17]

Having read an advertisement in the newspaper *France-Soir*, which 'announced that a major record company wanted to audition beginners', Françoise duly applied. This television and phonographic manufacturing company was Pathé-Marconi. It is about then that she revealed her mindset, stating that one should always expect the worst, in order 'to avoid being brought back down to earth with a thud'.[18] In short, she was far from confident. 'I do not like my voice', she said. 'I do not like what it reveals about my physical limitations.'[19]

In autumn 1961, French pianist André Bernot offered to give Françoise lessons in sight reading – the ability to play or perform a previously unseen piece of music simply by reading the score. She was currently in her first year, studying German at the Sorbonne University in Paris. In anticipation of Françoise attending another record company for a second audition, they chose a song by Elvis Presley entitled, 'I Gotta Know'. 'Accompanying me on the piano, André taught me how to start, stop, and pick up again where I should.'[20]

When Bernot judged that his student was ready, he presented the taped recording of the song to French music publisher and record producer Jacques Wolfsohn who, having heard Françoise sing in person, immediately offered her a contract with French record company *Disques Vogue* (founded in 1947) of which he was artistic director.

1. Hardy, Françoise, *The Despair of Monkeys and Other Trifles*, p.10.
2. Ibid, p.11.
3. Ibid, p.21.
4. Quinonero, Frédéric, *Françoise Hardy : Un Long Chant d'amour*, pp.39-40.
5. Hardy, Françoise, *The Despair of Monkeys and Other Trifles*, op. cit., p.22.
6. Beardsley, Eleanor, 'Françoise Hardy Remains France's National Treasure', NPR, 12 September 2018.

7. 'Pop Music': *The New Grove Dictionary of Music and Musicians*.
8. Hardy, Françoise, *The Despair of Monkeys and Other Trifles*, op. cit., p.22.
9. Soanes, Catherine and Angus Stevenson (Editors), *Oxford Dictionary of English*.
10. Moreland, Quinn, 'French Icon Françoise Hardy on the Music of Her Life', Pitchfork, 10 May 2018, online.
11. Hardy, Françoise, *The Despair of Monkeys and Other Trifles*, op. cit., p.23.
12. Ibid, p.23.
13. Ibid, p.24.
14. 'Falling for Françoise', A Falling Tree Production for BBC Radio 4, 2011.
15. Hardy, Françoise, *The Despair of Monkeys and Other Trifles*, op. cit., p.24.
16. Ibid, p.25.
17. Ibid, p.26.
18. Ibid, p.26.
19. Massenet, Ariane et Béatrice, *Mères et Fils : Ce que je voudrais te dire*, in Quinonero, Frédéric, *Françoise Hardy : Un Long Chant d'amour*, p.27.
20. Hardy, Françoise, *The Despair of Monkeys and Other Trifles*, op. cit., p.31.

7
The Road to Success!

Françoise's contract with *Disques Vogue*, which was for one year, was signed on 14 November 1961. It was in fact signed by Françoise's mother, because her daughter was still underage. 'I don't think I have ever been happier in my professional life than afterwards', she said, when she left the building and found herself 'in the street with [her] little guitar'.[1]

Charles Benarroch, percussionist with 'El Toro & The Cyclones', said of Françoise, 'I often saw her in the building, guitar in hand, shy and fearful, but something magical emanated from her. Everything was already in place, as if it had always been there'.[2]

In 1962, Françoise auditioned at the Petit Conservatoire de Mireille (otherwise known as the Petit Conservatoire de la Chanson), an academy for singers founded by French singer, composer, and actress Mireille Hartuck. Here, she performed the song *Madame Rose*, by Canadian country musician Patrick Norman (stage name of Yvon Éthier), in public.

Having heard her sing in front of her other students, Mireille subsequently said of Françoise 'that she knew immediately [that she] was destined to be someone'. Françoise was now enrolled in a class, with Mireille as her tutor.[3] 'Mireille played a big part in my life', said Françoise. 'She was the first person to trust me.' In fact, 'our relationship was reminiscent of that between mother and daughter', declared Françoise.[4]

As regards the music, said Françoise, Mireille was not merely concerned with 'the quality of what was being expressed', she also believed that the 'overall bearing, presentation', and 'body language' as displayed by the artist were important.[5]

'From this exchange ensued a long and solid friendship, born out of mutual respect', said French writer and biographer Frédéric Quinonero.[6]

Françoise contacted the record company *Disques Vogue*, having heard that the company was looking 'for a female counterpart' to French rock and roll and pop singer and actor Johnny Hallyday, who had just been signed and 'whose celebrity was growing'.[7] Meanwhile, Françoise was advised to 'take advantage of the summer vacation to work with a piano player on how to keep the beat [rhythm]'.[8] 'I was not even aware that a singer had to follow the rhythm, I just assumed that [the other] musicians kept up', she said![9]

In those early days, in respect of her own compositions, said Quinonero, Françoise 'composed her melodies whilst accompanying herself on the guitar, even though she could neither read nor write a score'. She 'cannot purport to be a songwriter and she resigns herself to co-writing her first songs with Roger Samyn', arranger, conductor and a member of the SACEM [Société des Auteurs, Compositeurs et Éditeurs de Musique, in English, Society of Authors, Composers, and Publishers of Music]'.[10]

On 25 April 1962, at Wolfsohn's suggestion, Françoise recorded her first record, the song *Oh! Oh! Chéri*, by US singer Bobby Lee Trammell and French songwriters Gilbert Guenet and Jean Setti ('Jil et Jan'). It was released in June 1962 on the *Disques Vogue* label).[11] However, she preferred the flipside of the record, *Tous les Garçons et les Filles* ('All the Boys and Girls'), composed by herself and Roger Samyn.

Her eponymous album (released in November 1962) quickly sold over 2 million copies! Further hits followed, such as *Mon Amie la rose*, released in 1964. She was now destined to feature regularly on the covers of the French language weekly news magazine *Paris Match* and other fashionable publications of the day.

When she heard the recording of *Tous les Garçons et les Filles* being broadcast on the privately-owned radio Europe No. 1, which broadcast to France, Switzerland and Belgium, said Françoise, 'I could hardly believe my ears and was overwhelmed by an indescribable joy'.[12] Within a few months, the song had sold millions of copies. 'I was incapable of realizing what had happened to me', declared Françoise.[13]

In respect of *Tous les Garçons et les Filles*, said Quinonero, 'At the beginning of 1963, half a million French households owned Françoise Hardy's record', and 'her cult song started to be exported abroad in its original version and was translated in several languages such as Italian, German and English'.[14]

Following the success of her third EP (extended play record), featuring the song *Ton Meilleur Ami* ('Your Best Friend', released 21 January 1963), lyrics by Françoise, music by Françoise and Samyn, Françoise declared: 'I must absolutely get away from the radio and the record player, in order to become a real entity for the thousands of young people who are turning me into a star before I even realize that I am an artist.'[15]

Françoise became 'more than a teen phenomenon. Her fans included: The Beatles, jazz trumpeter Miles Davis, and Mick Jagger who declared her his 'ideal woman'. While Bob Dylan dedicated a poem to her on the sleeve of his 1964 album, *Another Side of Bob Dylan*':[16]

> For Françoise Hardy
> At the Seine's edge
> A giant shadow
> Of Notre Dame
> Seeks t'grab my foot.
> Sorbonne students
> Whirl by
> On thin bicycles
> Swirlin' lifelike colours
> Of leather spin ...

French journalist and member of the Académie française (French Literary Academy) Bernard Pivot subsequently remarked insightfully, that, 'Françoise Hardy had something others did not possess or, if at all, only slightly: she had grace, a particular grace which heightened her obvious intelligence and which was going to make of her not an idol, but an icon of the world of song'.[17] How right he turned out to be!

Françoise summarized her attitude to music thus: 'I primarily like slow and sad melodies, those which rub salt in the wound. Not in a draining way but in an uplifting way, because it feels good when emotional pain becomes something beautiful: a beautiful text, a beautiful melody. I always seek to find a harrowing melody which will bring tears to my eyes, a melody so perfect that it becomes almost sacred.'[18]

Here, Françoise was echoing a universal truth: that great art often has its origins in trauma and sadness.

'The inspiration for my lyrics partially stems from my anxieties', Françoise admitted. 'In many songs, I touched upon the fear of not being good enough and of being abandoned for a woman theoretically a thousand times more interesting and attractive than I. Such a fear was not necessarily unfounded.'[19]

1. Hardy, Françoise, series of interviews for RTS.
2. Quinonero, Frédéric, interview with Charles Benarroch, June 2016, in Quinonero, Frédéric, *Françoise Hardy : Un Long Chant d'amour*, p.54.
3. Hardy, Françoise, *The Despair of Monkeys and Other Trifles*, p.27.
4. *L'Express*, 27 April 2000, in Quinonero, Frédéric, *Françoise Hardy : Un Long Chant d'amour*, p.46.
5. Hardy, Françoise, *The Despair of Monkeys and Other Trifles*, op. cit., p.28.
6. *L'Express*, 27 April 2000.
7. Hardy, Françoise, *The Despair of Monkeys and Other Trifles*, op. cit., p.28.
8. Ibid, p.29.
9. *Libération*, 4 April 2009, in Quinonero, Frédéric, *Françoise Hardy : Un Long Chant d'amour*, p.52.
10. Quinonero, Frédéric, *Françoise Hardy : Un Long Chant d'amour*, p.55.
11. Hardy, Françoise, *The Despair of Monkeys and Other Trifles*, op. cit., p.33.

12. Ibid, p.33.
13. Ibid, p.34.
14. Quinonero, Frédéric, *Françoise Hardy : Un Long Chant d'amour*, op. cit., p.93.
15. Françoise Hardy, Claude Dufresne, Je chante, donc je suis, in Quinonero, Frédéric, *Françoise Hardy : Un Long Chant d'amour*, p.69.
16. Fiegel, Eddi, 'Sixties sensation Françoise Hardy on her Lifetime in Music', Complete France, 24 December 2018.
17. *Le Journal de Dimanche*, 23 October 2008.
18. *Le Nouvel Observateur*, 9 October 2012, in Quinonero, Frédéric, *Françoise Hardy : Un Long Chant d'amour*, p.39.
19. *L'Express*, 23 May 2013, in Quinonero, Frédéric, *Françoise Hardy : Un Long Chant d'amour*, p.86.

8
1960: Romance with Jean-Marie Périer and further Success

When a famous French photographer to the stars named Jean-Marie Périer called at the family home with some photographs, the outcome was the kindling of a relationship with Françoise which, she said, 'went beyond simple flirting'.[1] Whereupon, at her mother's suggestion, she 'purchased her first flat, an attic studio on the fourth floor of 8 rue du Rocher', in Paris's Monceau district, 8th arrondissement, 'near the Gare Saint-Lazare'.[2] Furthermore, said Quinonero, 'the new millionaire songstress soon set up her mother and sister in a comfortable flat, 29 rue d'Anjou, close to her own home'.[3]

In the early 1970s, said Quinonero, Françoise left her studio, 8 rue du Rocher, 'to move into a three-room apartment on the fourth floor of 10 rue Saint-Louis-en-l'Île, a prestigious address on one of the two islands on the river Seine'.[4]

Meanwhile, Jean-Marie, lived on the rue du Faubourg Saint-Honoré, another enviable address in the 8th arrondissement, with his friend Régis Pagniez, a designer for French publishing executive Daniel Filipacchi. However, every time Jean-Marie left for foreign reporting assignments, said Françoise, 'This would plunge me into a state of distress comparable to the devastation I felt when the Orient Express tore me away from my mother'.[5]

On the positive side, said Françoise, Jean-Marie 'taught me to love the cinema' and to realize 'the importance of aesthetics'. He also taught her 'how to carry' herself 'and to dress' and he gave her advice 'on social skills'.[6] He also took Françoise to Corsica to meet his paternal relations and persuaded her to buy a plot of land there with the idea of building a house on it.[7]

When he was instructed to take photographs of Bulgarian-French singer and actress Sylvie Vartan, Françoise was 'initially haunted by the thought that Jean-Marie would fall in love with her'.[8] All was not well in the 'Garden of Eden', said Françoise. 'My inferiority complexes, which I tried my best to hide from Jean-Marie, poisoned our relationship.' She also found their long separations increasingly hard to bear. This was a time when, as her popularity increased, she herself was 'travelling a lot to take part in either major television shows, or in festivals and concert tours'. Françoise felt as if her 'personal life was on hold'. She said 'I hid out in my hotel bathrooms, as generally their acoustics were excellent. With the help of my guitar, I tirelessly attempted to put my needs and grief into music'.[9] This was to be a feature of Françoise's entire life.

'The condescension of certain French journalists toward the singers of my generation, all from humble backgrounds, shocks me more today than at the time I had to deal with it', said Françoise five decades later. She referred specifically to French TV presenter Denise Glaser, 'whose affectation was like a caricature' and who 'gave herself superior airs and made no effort to come down to your level'; and to French journalist Pierre Dumayet, 'who made me undergo a kind of humiliating exam intended to reveal my lack of a literary education'.[10]

Meanwhile, said Françoise, two of her compositions, *Et même* ('However much', 1964) and *Dans le monde entier* ('All Over the World', 1965) 'were adapted into English and made it onto "Top of the Pops". However, the English language press was much less interested in me as a singer than they were as an ambassadress of French style'.[11] Françoise's favourite stylist was French fashion designer André Courrèges, and she set her heart on one of his creations, 'an immaculate ensemble of form-fitting pants and tunic with matching white ankle boots'. Françoise admired the 'disarming simplicity, human warmth, and normalcy' of André and his wife Coqueline, which set them apart from 'the usual great couturiers'.[12]

On the advice of French pop singer Richard Anthony, Françoise travelled to London, 'to record under the guidance of the talented Charles Blackwell [British record producer], whose orchestrations finally brought the best out of [her] songs, or to perform in the prestigious cabaret at the Savoy hotel'.[13] The reason that she went to London to make her records, she said, was 'because [she] was unhappy with French musicians'.[14]

Against her better judgement, Françoise was persuaded to appear in two films. The first, *Château en Suède*, was filmed in France, Lapland, and Stockholm, Sweden. The second, *Une Balle au cœur*, was filmed in Greece. About the time she was there, Françoise said: 'I lived only for the moment when I would see Jean-Marie again. So, while I felt lonelier and worse than ever, my need for love gradually turned toward a charming young man who was part of the shoot. This was nothing other than a gasp of life, but it triggered the deterioration of my relationship with Jean-Marie and the end of our love'.[15]

Italian bass player Hermès Alesi explained how deeply involved Françoise's mother was in her daughter's professional life at that time. Said he, 'I went on tour with Françoise for two years, from 1964', and for all of that time, 'we were in constant touch with Madeleine Hardy regarding the tours. She was in charge of the organisation. She was very bossy, things had to be done her way. She treated her daughter like a child, even though Françoise knew exactly what she wanted in spite of never being satisfied herself'.[16] Self-criticism and perfectionism were Françoise's trademark!

In 1964, *Mon Amie la rose*, ['The Rose'] by French composer Cécile Caulier and Canadian conductor Jacques Lacome, sung by Françoise, was released by *Disques Vogue*. The song, with its themes of the transitory nature of life and love and of the need to hope, appealed to Françoise enormously. However, said Quinonero, 'it was really not easy to convince her entourage, particularly Jacques Wolfsohn who did not believe that such a grim subject could appeal to a vast audience. In spite of all this, the song became a success abroad, both in French and in its English version', *The Rose*.[17] Françoise was nothing if not persistent when she saw potential in a song!

1. Hardy, Françoise, *The Despair of Monkeys and Other Trifles*, p.36.
2. Quinonero, Frédéric, *Françoise Hardy : Un Long Chant d'amour*, p.76.
3. Ibid, p.77.
4. Ibid, p.211.
5. Hardy, Françoise, *The Despair of Monkeys and Other Trifles*, op. cit., p.37.
6. Ibid, p.37.
7. Ibid, p.38.
8. Ibid, p.39.
9. Ibid, p.42.
10. Ibid, p.46.
11. Ibid, p.47.
12. Ibid, p.47.
13. Ibid, pp.47-8.
14. 'Falling for Françoise', A Falling Tree Production for BBC Radio 4, 2011.
15. Hardy, Françoise, *The Despair of Monkeys and Other Trifles*, op. cit., pp.51-2.
16. Quinonero, Frédéric, interview with Hermès Alesi, May 2016.
17. Quinonero, Frédéric, *Françoise Hardy : Un Long Chant d'amour*, op. cit., p.105.

9
About Jacques Dutronc

Jacques Dutronc was born on 28 April 1943 at 67 rue de Provence in Paris's 9th arrondissement. He was therefore 9 months older than Françoise. Jacques' parents were Pierre, a manager for the state-run Office of Coal Distribution, and Madeleine (née Sounier).

Jacques was educated at the private Catholic Lycée Rocroy-Saint-Léon, 106 rue du Faubourg-Poissonnière in the 10th arrondissement. However, matters did not go well. For mathematics, he said, he had a teacher who could not stand him. This, he thought, may have been because he [Jacques] always smelt of tobacco. Chain smoking was a feature of Jacques' life!

One day, his teacher asked him to draw a line on the blackboard, but when he reached the edge of the board, she asked him to carry on along the wall until he reached the door. Then she asked him to open the door, whereupon she said to him, 'Goodbye!'. In other words, he had been expelled.

However, said Jacques, even though he had left school without his baccalaureate, he was not entirely dismayed because this event had furnished him with a nice story to tell his friends![1]

Jacques subsequently attended the École de la rue Blanche (a school for the performing arts), and then the École professionnelle de dessin industriel where, from 1959, he studied graphic design. Meanwhile, he joined a small band as a guitar player.

Having passed an examination in Art Deco (the predominant decorative art style of the 1920s and 1930s COD), Jacques became seriously ill for a period of 6 months. During this time, he decided to improve his skills in music and guitar playing.[2]

In 1960, Jacques as guitarist formed his own band, together with schoolfriend Hadi Kalafate as bassist, French percussionist Charles 'Charlot' Benarroch (later replaced with André Crudo), and French songwriter and musician Daniel Dray as vocalist. In

1961, the band auditioned for Jacques Wolfsohn at *Disques Vogue*, who signed them and gave them the name 'El Toro et les Cyclones'. The group released two singles, *L'Oncle John* and *Le Vagabond*. However, it was disbanded in 1962 when Jacques was called up for 18 months of mandatory military service.[3]

1. *Dutronc, Jacques, 'Je préfère les animaux aux dames', Interview 1971, YouTube.
2. Ibid.
3. 'Jacques Dutronc', *Wikipedia*.

10
1966: Françoise Hardy and Jacques Dutronc

When Jacques Dutronc returned home to Paris in 1964, having completed his military service, Jacques Wolfsohn 'recruited him as his assistant at *Éditions Alpha*', a record production company of which he, Wolfsohn, was founder and director. Meanwhile, Jacques 'was hired as a guitarist in Eddy Mitchell's orchestra [French singer and actor, stage name of Claude Moine], for a series of gigs at the Golf Drouot nightclub'.[1] In this capacity, he co-wrote songs for artists such as French singer and actress Zouzou (stage name of Danièle Ciarlet), Polish singer Cléo (stage name of Joanna Klepko), and Françoise Hardy, who was also on the *Disques Vogue* label. "His close-cropped hair, pimply skin, and enormous glasses at this time were hardly flattering', said Françoise.[2]

Jacques Dutronc 'was not a complete stranger to me', said Françoise, 'as I had covered a song of his in 1963 that I liked a lot'. This was *Le Temps d'amour* ('The Time of Love', *Disques Vogue*), music by Jacques Dutronc, lyrics by Lucien Morisse and André Salvet.

When Jacques was 'mentioned to me as a possible guitar player for a concert tour', Françoise continued, 'he remained evasive'. This was at a time when 'he had not yet become a celebrity'. However, *Et moi, et moi, et moi,* music by Jacques Dutronc, lyrics by the French journalist, writer, and lyricist Jacques Lanzmann 'was bombarding the airwaves'.

Jacques was engaged to be married. However, 'he cancelled his wedding several days before it was to be celebrated'. With hindsight, said Françoise, this 'should have aroused my suspicions'. Could the reason have been 'a reflexive need to flee from any form of commitment?' How right she turned out to be! Nevertheless, now that they were both single – i.e. unattached -, she said, 'We often went out together, starting in the fall of 1966'.[3]

Meanwhile, Françoise had just returned from Milan, Italy, where the last sequence of the sports drama film *Grand Prix* (released 21 December 1966) had been shot, at the nearby Monza motor racing circuit. In the film, Françoise had played the minor part of 'Lisa'. 'My insipid lines could have been counted on the fingers of one hand', she said.[4]

Quinonero described how 'the two artists', Jacques and Françoise, 'who shared the same record label [*Disques Vogue*], had developed the habit of going out together along with their artistic director [Jacques Wolfsohn]. All three were then single: Wolfsohn had just divorced his wife, Dutronc had left his fiancée a few days before their wedding because she could not deal with the thought of sharing her life with a musician, let alone a singer, and Françoise was desperately trying to get over her clandestine relationship with [British actor] Peter McEnery'.[5]

In those early days, Françoise described Jacques as 'a deeply annoying creature: he never totally opens up and turns everything which is important to you into a joke. You really begrudge him that at first, but when you understand that he also makes light of his own hardships to save you getting bored, he becomes quite endearing. You realize that he is more intelligent and sensitive than he is willing to let you see'.[6] In other words, Françoise had the sensitivity to realize that deep down, Jacques was a troubled person. Subsequently, said Quinonero, 'the two artists became inseparable'.[7]

Françoise explained how her 'own inferiority complexes' initially prevented her 'from seeing his, which were as deep, and which [she] discovered a little at a time. [Hers] were reflected in [her] excessive submissiveness; his in his evasiveness'.[8] Again, this was very perceptive of Françoise, because no one would have guessed this from the persona which Jacques presented in public.

Jacques, for his part, 'was very impressed by Françoise', said French composer, actor, and bass guitarist Hadi Kalafate, 'both because of her beauty and her stardom. She became famous before he did. And she did not completely realize everything she radiated, and how it could be inhibiting for a shy guy like Jacques'.[9]

1. Quinonero, Frédéric, *Françoise Hardy : Un Long Chant d'amour*, p.87.
2. Hardy, Françoise, *The Despair of Monkeys and Other Trifles*, op. cit., p.57.
3. Ibid, pp.57-8.
4. Ibid, p.53.
5. Quinonero, Frédéric, *Françoise Hardy : Un Long Chant d'amour*, op. cit., p.154.
6. *Salut les Copains*, No. 62.
7. Quinonero, Frédéric, *Françoise Hardy : Un Long Chant d'amour*, op. cit., p.155.
8. Domain, Valérie, *Femmes de, Filles de : Portraits de femmes d'influence*.
9. Kalafate, Hadi, interview with Frederic Quinonero, July 2016.

11
Further Success

As already mentioned, it was in September 1967 that Françoise commenced a relationship with Jacques Dutronc. During the last quarter of that year, said Quinonero, Françoise's new songs were produced by her own company, 'which she named "Asparagus", as a nod to the nickname of "Grande Asperge" ['Large Asparagus'] which she was often given'.[1] This was hardly flattering, considering what a physically beautiful creature Françoise was!

In 1968, said Quinonero, 'rumours had been circulating for many months' that Françoise 'intended leaving the stage' i.e. as a performer.[2] Said she, 'I have never liked the stage because I was vocally limited. And rhythmically also. I could not rely on my voice. There was always the risk of a weakness, a wrong note. And I hated travelling'.[3] In fact, said Françoise, 'My first and only ambition had been to record, and this was the only thing that truly interested me. The stage, the photo sessions, the programs, the interviews were all so much drudgery that I really could do without'.[4]

Françoise spent three weeks in England, from 22 April to 14 May 1968, where she stayed at London's Savoy Hotel in the Strand, a favourite meeting place for London society. Said Quinonero, 'The place was so exclusive that Jacques Dutronc, who had come with his mate Hadi Kalafate, was thrown out onto the street!' Said Kalafate himself:

'Jacques and I were on holiday in Marrakesh [Morocco], at La Mamounia. From there, we went directly to London, via Paris. Once at the Savoy, a bit scruffy and out of it, we were singled out by the doormen. Of course, they had no idea who Jacques was, because he was unknown in England, and as much as he kept screaming that he was Françoise Hardy's partner, they replied to him something along the lines of "Yes, yes, and we are Elvis Presley!". The doormen were gigantic, more than 1.80 m in height, and as we were both quite short, they literally grabbed us by the scruff of the neck and threw us out like trash! It was violent.'

'Immediately afterwards, Wolfsohn arrived and, as he spoke perfect English, he settled the matter by confirming that Jacques was indeed Françoise's partner. So finally, we were able to stay at the hotel. But Jacques was not allowed to sleep in the same room as Françoise, because they were not married.'

As for Françoise, 'she was given armfuls of flowers every night'.[5] On her return to Paris on 15 May 1968, said Quinonero: 'Just as the trade-unions were turning the student revolt into an unprecedented social movement (unbeknown to the political powers), Françoise Hardy opened the first international exhibition of diamonds at Clerc jewellers, place de l'Opéra. She was wearing "the most expensive minidress in the world", a Paco Rabanne [Spanish fashion designer] creation of square and rectangular gold plates embedded with diamonds (nine kilos of gold and three hundred carats of diamonds), linked together with metal rivets and rings.'[6]

Sensational as this outfit may have appeared, it was completely impractical, not least because of its weight and inflexibility!

1. Quinonero, Frédéric, *Françoise Hardy : Un Long Chant d'amour*, p.169.
2. Ibid, p.177.
3. *Paris Match*, No. 3281.
4. Hardy, Françoise, *The Despair of Monkeys and Other Trifles*, p.81.
5. Quinonero, Frédéric, interview with Hadi Kalafate, July 2016.
6. Quinonero, Frédéric, *Françoise Hardy : Un Long Chant d'amour*, op. cit., p.181.

12
Literature: Some Favourite Authors

Said Françoise, 'Generally, I am passionate about anything to do with true love. Perfect love. My favourite films and books are all about it'.[1]

When Françoise was in Bavaria filming *Le Gai Savoir* ('The Joy of Learning', released 28 June 1969) directed by Franco-Swiss filmmaker Jean-Pierre Léaud, said Quinonero, Françoise 'preferred to stay alone in the tranquillity of her bedroom, in order to continue tackling the works of Proust'.[2]

In his novels, French novelist Marcel Proust (1871-1922) was concerned with childhood influences, the discovery of art, social changes, as well as a psychological understanding of literature, memory and time, its unreality and reversibility: themes which would have greatly appealed to Françoise!

Françoise regarded *Le Petit Prince* (1943), a novella by French aristocrat and writer Antoine de Saint-Exupéry, as one of the greatest masterpieces of literature. This is the story of a young prince who visited various planets, including Earth, and it addresses all the themes that were dearest to Françoise's heart: loneliness, friendship, love and loss. 'It says everything which matters to me in the most delicate way possible', she declared.[3]

In 2011 Françoise declared, 'You know, my favourite writer, and I read him again and again, is Henry James. When I read a good novel by Henry James I feel as happy as I can be.' She laughed. 'I forget everything which is terrible in our world.'[4] In other words, this is how Françoise transported herself into a safe and joyous environment.

Henry James (1843-1916) was a US novelist who became a naturalized British citizen in 1915. In his novels, James was concerned with the impact of European civilisation on the USA, the 'New World'.⁵

1. *Télérama*, No. 3277, in Quinonero, Frédéric, *Françoise Hardy : Un Long Chant d'amour*, p.335.
2. Ibid, p.173.
3. *Astrologie Naturelle*, No. 2, April 1998.
4. 'Falling for Françoise', A Falling Tree Production for BBC Radio 4, 2011.
5. Edel, Leon, 'Henry James: American Writer', *Britannica*.

13
A Young, Joyful, and Vivacious Françoise

In April 1970, the song *Effeuille-moi le cœur* ('Pull the petals of my heart'), for which Françoise wrote the lyrics, was released. In the video, Françoise is seen at her most charming and alluring: sitting at her typewriter, her head in her hands, her guitar in the corner of the room and piles of crumpled paper at her feet as she attempts in vain to compose a song! And here she is, hand over mouth, as she attempts to suppress a giggle; playfully brushing her hair with her hand and flicking it back with a turn of the head; making funny faces at the camera and smiling broadly! She was aged 26 at the time, and her happiness, wit, and sense of humour shine through![1]

In that same year of 1970, Françoise appeared on German television. She brought along with her to the interview a shy and retiring young man who was 18 months her junior. This was Patrick Modiano. Françoise had met Patrick a month previously at the funeral of a lady who, it transpired, had been both her and his wet nurse (woman employed to suckle another woman's child[2]). So, she and Patrick were 'milk cousins' she said laughingly.

Françoise described Patrick as 'a famous French author', and she had 'read a lot about him in the press'. Both were interested in the concepts of emptiness, loss, and identity, themes which were reflected in Patrick's books. In 2014, he was awarded the Nobel Prize in Literature.

For the occasion, Françoise was attired in a russet-coloured blouse, white slacks, and very high stilettos. Her flowing locks literally shone. Completely at ease, she was at her charming and scintillating best. One of the most fabulous flowers on the planet was in full bloom!

The first question put to Françoise by the female interviewer was, what did she most like to do? 'To sleep', Françoise replied in German. And second? 'To eat'. Smiles all round! As the interview progressed, Françoise became more and more expressive and animated, gesticulating with her arms and hands to make her points.

When Patrick was asked by the interviewer why he thought Françoise had been so successful, and why she was idolised by the French people, he replied, 'because she is beautiful, intelligent, talented and sensitive, but most of all because the stars shone brightly on her'. With each new adjective, Françoise's body language revealed that she was embarrassed at being showered with such praise from her friend. Her nervous smile turned to a giggle, and then to outright and uncontrollable laughter, as she blushed and repeatedly covered her mouth with her hand!

Finally, she sang delightfully in German the song *Was mach' ich ohne dich?* ('It Hurts to Say Goodbye?')

Alas, in the future, this carefree and joyous demeanour on the part of Françoise would be on display less and less.[3]

It happened that when Françoise was in London and leaving a nightclub, she was spotted by US film and TV director John Frankenheimer, who immediately decided that she 'would be perfect as one of the characters in a film he was preparing about Formula 1 motor racing.[4] Grand *Prix* was filmed from May to September 1966 and released on 21 December.

1. Hardy, Françoise, *Effeuille-moi le cœur*, Arte, April 1970.
2. Stevenson, A., and Waite, M., *Concise Oxford English Dictionary*.
3. Hardy, Françoise, German Television: *Was mach' ich ohne dich?* ('It Hurts to Say Goodbye?'), 1970. 4. Hardy, Françoise, *The Despair of Monkeys and Other Trifles*, p.53.

14
1971: An Interview with Jacques Dutronc

In an interview that he gave in 1971, Jacques appeared in a dark suit and bow tie. 'Suave' and debonair' were probably the epithets that suited him best. In other words, he was charming, seemingly confident, and elegant in both manner and attire which was his trademark. He was also fluent, with all the facts at his fingertips, animated and at times humorous, answering the questions put to him sincerely and honestly, without the sarcasm and showing off which sometimes characterized him. Meanwhile, a cigarette or very large cigar was never far from his lips!

From the mid-1960s, Jacques co-wrote songs for various artists, including Françoise Hardy. By this means, he said, he hoped to seduce her. Jacques might have used the word 'woo' ('courtiser') meaning 'to gain the love of';[1] or 'court' ('faire la cour à') meaning to become involved with romantically, typically with the intention of marrying'.[2] But instead, he used the word 'seduce' ('séduire'), meaning 'to entice into sexual activity'.[3] If he were to be successful, Jacques was asked, did he intend to live with Françoise and to marry her? Whereupon Jacques refused to answer. This is significant because it suggests that marriage was not his intention, at any rate at that early stage.

Instead, Jacques asked of the interviewer, 'Do you not read the newspapers?' According to them, he said dryly, he and Françoise had already married, then divorced, then married again, and then divorced again, etc., etc.! He declared that he himself was against marriage, on the grounds that a person does not require witnesses when he or she decides whether to live with somebody. In his view, it was a private matter between the two people concerned. Weddings were good only for presents, and for mitigating tax. He mentioned a lady friend of his who had married and received 'sumptuous presents for her wedding'. Did Jacques say this in jest? No, his body language indicated that he did not. This was not a 'throw away' line intended to amuse. It was said in all seriousness, which reinforces the notion that marriage was definitely not on the Dutronc agenda.

Jacques spoke about his period of compulsory military service, for 18 months during 1962 and 1963, when he played his guitar for the officers during their parties. After his time in the army, he returned to Paris and worked with Eddy Mitchell. But he continued to compose melodies for Françoise Hardy.

When somebody gave him the opportunity to sing, said Jacques, that was how his singing career began.[4] Jacques' first studio album, eponymously entitled *Jacques Dutronc*, was released in December 1966 (*Disques Vogue*).

Asked about animals, Jacques confessed that he preferred them to ladies. But animals and ladies are alike in that they are both capricious ('capricieux') and elegant ('élégants'). At home in the country, he disclosed that he had kept two cheetahs, and he was very sad when one of them died.

When Jacques said that he regarded marriage as unnecessary, this may simply have been that he disliked 'red tape' and fuss. On the other hand, it may have indicated an unwillingness to commit to a relationship. Or he may have felt that marriage was not required as a proof of love. Which of the two was true? Only time would tell.

1. Stevenson, A., and Waite, M., *Concise Oxford English Dictionary*.
2. Ibid.
3. Ibid.
4. *Dutronc, Jacques, 'Je préfère les animaux aux dames', Interview 1971, YouTube.

15
Getting to Know Jacques Better; Peter McEnery

Françoise and Jacques first performed together in public in October 1966, in a television special entitled 'Françoise Hardy Blues', directed by French television and radio director Jean-Christophe Averty. They performed *Mini-Mini-Mini* (lyrics by Jacques Dutronc, music by Jacques Lanzmann) with Jacques singing and Françoise, attired in a mini skirt which showed off her beautiful legs to perfection, posing; and *Les Garçons* (a parody of the song *Les Playboys*, lyrics by Jacques Lanzmann, music by Jacques Dutronc) in which they both sang and danced, and as they did so, she tapped him playfully on the head! Both songs were co-written by Jacques Dutronc and Jacques Lanzmann and released in October 1966 (*Disques Vogue*). In those early days of their romance, Françoise looked serenely happy.

However, had she but known it, the omens were not good. Said Kalafate, 'Jacques is unable to live with a partner. They rarely had dinner together, just the two of them, him and Françoise. He always had to invite someone [else, also]. Given his personality, which I know very well since we went to school together, it was impossible for him to have dinner alone with anyone, particularly a woman. He is such an introvert that there simply has to be a third person to avoid too much intimacy on his part and to compensate for his lack of confidence'.[1]

One evening, when Italian-French actor and singer Yves Montand had planned to take Françoise out to dinner, 'he had to cancel', said Quinonero, 'because of a last-minute emergency. But she still went out, with another knight in shining armour. By pure coincidence, she found herself in the same hip [fashionable] King's Road establishment as the English actor Peter McEnery, whom she had discovered the previous day at the cinema, in *La Curée* ['The Game is Over'].'

This was French screenwriter, film director, and producer Roger Vadim's latest film (released 22 June 1966).

Françoise found McEnery 'charming. She walked up to his table to introduce herself and fell under his spell! Later, when it was time to leave, he came to see her and suggested that they meet again. Nothing was holding her back'. Her love for Périer had 'lasted until the day [she] realized that [she] could be interested in another man', said Françoise. As for Périer, 'When you only see each other five or six days a month, you are madly in love with each other until saturation. After that, all that remains is a deep affection'.[2] In other words, the romance had burnt itself out.

However, said Quinonero, Françoise 'soon became disillusioned' with Peter McEnery: 'The handsome Englishman was not free nor willing to settle. But she decided to live the adventure to the full and to make the most of every moment she was allowed with him, even if the relationship turned out to be one-sided, and no matter how painful it would be to wake up from this gilded dream'.[3]

Meanwhile, Françoise's relationship with McEnery had been kept a secret, said Quinonero: 'She hardly uttered the name of her lover during interviews, and if so only to justify her new-found passion for the English theatre and particularly for Shakespeare, given that Peter McEnery was a member of the Royal Shakespeare Company. The press only talked about her break-up from Jean-Marie Périer, which she had instigated. And if both parties gave the idea of an amicable parting, Françoise Hardy admitted later that the experience was not without collateral damage.'

Said Françoise, 'This was the first time I went through the ordeal of causing an individual who I'd been most close to for several years to suffer, and I realized that it is less painful to leave someone than to have someone leave you'.[4] In other words, although she did what she felt she had to do, Françoise was concerned for McEnery's feelings, as well as for her own.

When the producers of *Grand Prix* invited Françoise to the USA, she fulfilled a promise by contacting Jessica Waters, a fellow actress from the film. 'After that, the telephone never stopped ringing.' She was photographed by US fashion and portrait photographer Richard Avedon, and the photographs, which she said were 'superb', were duly published in the American edition of *Vogue* magazine.[5] It was during her time in New York that Françoise was invited to lunch with Spanish surrealist painter Salvador Dali.

Having returned to Paris, said Françoise, she suffered with 'chronic digestive problems', and also 'had the beginnings of a nervous breakdown for the first and last time in [her] life'. She said: I would 'sometimes burst out weeping. Nothing excited me, but I had no inhibitions either. This made it possible for me to telephone Jacques Dutronc, confusedly viewing him as my life preserver.'[6]

On 20 April 1967, in a speech at the National Assembly, French Prime Minister Georges Pompidou mentioned Jacques's name and quoted from the song *Le Cactus* (lyrics by Jacques Lanzmann, music by Jacques Dutronc).[7] Jacques and Françoise were subsequently invited to the Élysée Palace, official residence of the President of the French Republic, to sing at a soirée for the Prime Minister and his guests, one of whom was French actress, singer, and model Brigitte Bardot. However, said Françoise, Jacques, 'who never did what was expected of him, and who seemed to take everything as an opportunity for mockery, started singing at 78 rpm, in other words at top speed. This cast a pall over the room'.[8]

By his action, Jacques had shown a total lack of respect for the assembled guests, but also for Françoise. Nonetheless, when Françoise subsequently saw Jacques on her television screen, she said, 'From that day, I was won over, I wanted to understand this enigmatic individual'.[9]

In June 1967 Jacques declared, 'I hate women who sleep next to you, who are there, with their lukewarm breath, like a sort of Velcro fastening. Because me, at night, I fart and I throw socks around'.[10]

Jacques had previously sent Françoise a postcard, she said, which was signed '"Your future fiancé", or something like that. [She] did not take this at all seriously, given his facetious nature and the total absence of any signals from him when [they] went out in groups of three or more'.[11] This was a highly significant comment on the part of Françoise, in the light of what was to follow.

Nevertheless, the two of them were subsequently much in each other's company. They worked for the same record company, and they were also 'scheduled on the same prime-time shows'. 'Little by little, said Françoise: 'I fell under the spell of not only his pale blue eyes but of his disconcerting personal style – provocative, sometimes cynical, always mysterious - behind which I liked to imagine lurked a great sensitivity as well as a great fragility.'[12]

Françoise was well read. Was she aware of a novel by her namesake poet and novelist, Thomas Hardy (1840-1928) entitled *A Pair of Blue Eyes* (published in 1873)? This described a love triangle between Elfride Swancourt, a beautiful young woman with eyes as 'blue as autumn distance', and her two suitors Stephen Smith and Henry Knight. The novel was inspired by Hardy's courtship of Emma Gifford, whom he met in 1870 and married in 1874, with disastrous consequences. Emma, said Hardy, had 'strikingly blue eyes'.

Françoise frequently stated that she regarded 'the real Jacques' as a 'sensitive' person[13] with 'an inferiority complex'[14] who was 'hiding an internal pain behind a provoking, nonchalant, or even cruel façade'.[15] and the fact that she saw him in this light clearly brought all her caring instincts to the fore. However, the harsh reality for her was, as she herself acknowledged, that 'nothing gave [her] grounds to assume even an ounce of reciprocity for [her] growing attraction'.[16]

When Françoise's car broke down and she was given a lift by Jacques, she 'hoped deep down that he would take advantage of the situation'. She pretended to sleep but took the opportunity, as the vehicle swung round the bends in the road, 'to rub against him slightly'. But 'nothing happened'. Françoise admitted that this seemed to be 'mission impossible'[17] Surely by now, for her, the proverbial penny was beginning to drop?

A nephew of the Shah of Iran invited Françoise to that country, under the pretext of 'the inauguration of a discotheque baptised "Tous les Garcons et les Filles" but hoping all the while to impress her with his 'largesse'. However, she said, 'He did not yet know that friendship, like love, cannot be bought'.[18]

In summer 1967, said Françoise, her house in Corsica was almost finished. 'It was already more beautiful' than she had imagined in her 'wildest dreams'.[19] The 'house-warming party was attended by Jacques and 'several of his buddies'.[20] However, to her 'chagrin', Jacques 'had by his side the so-so [neither very good not very bad[21]] wife of another singer, who had been chasing him for some time and who I was positive had gotten what she was after. Despite all lack of clues, I had instinctively known for months that my attraction was shared.'[22]

It was a relief to Françoise when the woman 'left as quickly as she got there'.[23] This left her as the only female in the group, whereupon, she said, '[she] threw myself' into cooking, even though '[she] had never cooked in [her] life'.[24] But when alone in her room, she found herself 'despairing a little more each evening over the prospect that something would finally happen between Jacques and [her]. Whereupon Jacques Wolfsohn gave Françoise a piece of advice: 'Someone who had multiple love affairs like Dutronc, could only make [her] unhappy'.[25]

Françoise's own intuition, coupled with other indications, should have alerted her to the fact that this was a no-go situation. But as for Wolfsohn, she said, 'I paid no attention to his warnings'.

One evening, Françoise found herself alone with her 'heart's desire'. 'The man who hardly ever spoke talked to me for hours, and we ended up in bed, but I was so drunk that to my great regret, I cannot remember a thing.' The following day, Jacques wore a red shirt. It was only years later that Françoise learned that this had been a 'little conspiracy', a 'signal to his accomplices that the operation was a success'.[26] In other words, it had been contrived on the part of Jacques, and was not done out of love.

Did Jacques regard Françoise merely as an acquaintance, and if so, why did he not tell her as much? Or was he afraid of hurting her feelings? Or did he regard her primarily as a trophy, a trophy of the 'Monarch of the Glen'; someone he was simply stringing along? Only time would tell.

1. Interview with the author (Quinonero), June 2016, in Quinonero, Frédéric, *Françoise Hardy : Un Long Chant d'amour*, p.203.

2. *Elle*, No. 1090, p.143
3. Quinonero, Frédéric, *Françoise Hardy : Un Long Chant d'amour*, pp.142-3.
4. Hardy, Françoise, *The Despair of Monkeys and Other Trifles*, p.57.
5. Ibid, p.60.
6. Ibid, pp.60-1.
7. Quinonero, Frédéric, *Françoise Hardy : Un Long Chant d'amour*, op. cit., p.149.
8. Hardy, Françoise, *The Despair of Monkeys and Other Trifles*, p.73.
9. *Salut les Copains*, No. 62, September 1967.
10. *Libération*, 28 February 2000, in Quinonero, Frédéric, *Françoise Hardy : Un Long Chant d'amour*, pp.201-2.
11. Hardy, Françoise, *The Despair of Monkeys and Other Trifles*, p.61.
12. Ibid, p.61.
13. Ibid, p.135.
14. Ibid, p.161.
15. Hardy, Françoise, *Chansons sur toi et nous*, p.102.
16. Hardy, Françoise, *The Despair of Monkeys and Other Trifles*, op. cit., p.61.
17. Ibid, p.62.
18. Ibid, p.63.
19. Ibid, p.66.
20. Ibid, p.66.
21. Stevenson, A., and Waite, M., *Concise Oxford English Dictionary*.
22. Hardy, Françoise, *The Despair of Monkeys and Other Trifles*, pp.66-7.
23. Ibid, p.66.
24. Ibid, p.67.
25. Ibid, p.68.
26. Ibid, p.68.

16
Françoise develops her music

Françoise stated that her (serious) relationship with Jacques commenced in September 1967.[1] She and Jacques now began seeing each other 'around once a week and generally went out to dinner at a wonderful small restaurant on the Île de la Cité, La Colombe. [They] would sometimes go back to his place after, but more often to [hers]. Jacques lived in an apartment 'on the top storey' of his parents' home at 67 rue de Provence.[2]

When French singer-songwriter Jean-Pierre Sabar, whom Françoise described as an 'exceptionally gifted pianist', agreed to be her accompanist on the piano, this, she said, 'was a gift from heaven'. Furthermore, singing on stage for her now became 'much more enjoyable'. Sabar's 'piano playing and the choruses he concocted carried [her] rhythmically better than anybody [she had] been forced to make do with until then'.[3]

On a visit to South Africa in spring 1968, Françoise met Dr Christiaan Barnard, who had performed the world's first heart transplant operation on 3 December 1967.[4] Whilst in South Africa, her portrait was painted by Russian painter Vladimir Trechikoff (1913-2006). An oil on canvas, he entitled it 'Portrait of the Singer Françoise Hardy: Rainy Day'. Trechikoff appears to have had an incredible insight, because here is his subject, looking out of the window on a rainy day, as the raindrops, which resemble tears, appear to trickle down the window.

In that year of 1968, in Brazil, Françoise's interpreter was Lena, who was 'caring, kind, generous, intelligent, and wise'. Françoise declared that Lena would become her 'best friend'.[5] Her next visit would be to the Belgian Congo.[6]

When her artistic agent Lionel Roc suggested to Françoise that she 'stop performing live for a while' and spend her time recording, she was delighted. 'My first and only ambition had been to record and this was the only thing that truly interested me. The stage, the photo sessions, the [TV] programmes, the interviews were all so much drudgery that I really could do without.'[7] She was also 'very relieved at putting an end to a nomadic life that absolutely did not suit [her] and harmed [her] vocal abilities'.[8]

French musician Bernard Estardy was 'director and sound mixer' at Studio CBE, a recording studio located in Paris's rue Championnet. 'There was no one like him when it came to adjusting the mix in the headsets, in which the orchestral balance and vocal playback became so magical that every singer who has worked with him remembers it fondly. This was the first time I felt so much pleasure and ease when singing, and I recorded regularly at [Studio] CBE until I met [French singer-songwriter] Michel Berger in 1973.'[9]

1. Locoge, Benjamin, 'Françoise Hardy: Mes chansons m'aidaient à supporter mes douleurs ['My Songs Helped me to Endure My Pains'], *Paris Match*, 23 March 2021.
2. Hardy, Françoise, *The Despair of Monkeys and Other Trifles*, p.69.
3. Ibid, p.74.
4. Ibid, p.75.
5. Ibid, p.77.
6. Ibid, p.80.
7. Ibid, p.81.
8. Ibid, p.81.
9. Ibid, p.87.

17
Françoise and Jacques: Meltdown!

What was Françoise's ideal of a perfect personality? Perhaps that possessed by French singer-songwriter and poet Georges Brassens, who, she said, 'she worshiped more than anyone else. He beamed intelligence, humour, sensitivity, and kindness. You simply had to like him'.[1]

In late 1968, Françoise's dear friend, Lena arrived in Paris from Brazil. She said: 'Her arrival was a blessing for me insofar as only her enlightened friendship helped me bear the progressive deterioration of my relationship with Jacques.' Jacques' attitude towards her had changed, said Françoise. He had become 'increasingly unavailable', and 'cancelled [their] dates at the last minute'. Furthermore, the following year, 1969, she said, 'marked the start of this destructive routine which went on for several years'.

For example, at about this time, Jacques asked Françoise to bring back some 'big band records' from England, where she was scheduled to appear on television. But on her return home to Paris, where he had agreed to take her out for dinner, Françoise discovered that he had gone to Clermont-Ferrand. In a rage, she said, 'I took the Cartier brooch with turquoise and diamonds that Jacques bought me', and 'furiously stomped on it'.

Soon after, at the suggestion of Jacques Wolfsohn, her artistic director at the *Disques Vogue* record company, Françoise went to see Jacques Dutronc perform in cabaret at Paris's Les Têtes de l'Art restaurant: 'It was like a nightmare. The beautiful Nathalie Delon [French actress], about whom I heard Jacques say jokingly on radio RTL [French commercial radio network] that he would do his best to replace her husband (French cinema superstar and heartthrob Alain Delon), was enthroned in the dressing room, absolutely radiant. Seeing my place had been taken, I beat a retreat.'

Nevertheless, when Jacques invited Françoise to Paris's La Cloche d'Or restaurant, she accepted the invitation. But: 'The next morning, when I was saying goodbye, he didn't even favour me with a single word, as if nothing had happened, as if it did not matter to him one way or the other if we saw each other again or not. This was the point I hit rock bottom and did something that was entirely contrary to my nature. I went to Castel's [the Paris nightclub Club Castel] that very evening and picked up the first young man who came my way. It was stupid, pathetic, and solved nothing. But people will do anything when they are in despair.'

In order to 'learn the innermost reasons' for her 'personal problems', Françoise took a course in psychology, and she also underwent hypnosis. She now relocated to a 'three-room place' on the Île Saint-Louis, 'a sublime haven of beauty, where I never dreamed I would one day live'. Finally, she signed a second contract with *Disques Vogue* for a five-year term.

Meanwhile, 'Lena and I got along so well', said Françoise, 'that she left her job as a sales assistant to become my secretary/assistant'.

In that year of 1969, Françoise travelled to Las Vegas, USA to see Elvis Presley perform at the Hilton International Hotel. This left her with a 'dazzling memory'. However, she said, 'If I had one complaint', it was about Presley's 'atrociously kitschy [i.e. in poor taste] outfit'. By contrast, when Françoise was introduced by Lena to her compatriot, the Brazilian singer, guitarist and songwriter, Tuca (given name Valeniza Zagni da Silva), who was currently based in Paris, she 'instantly fell madly in love with her as an artist and as a friend', she said.

In summer 1970, Jacques invited Françoise to join him and his band at a house which he was renting in Grasse, on the French Riviera. However. 'I had not yet realized', she said 'that there was no place for me in his bubble of pals, where playing the fool was the rule. Not that my presence could disrupt the homogeneity of this little world in which I was a foreigner. Jacques needed it because he felt more at ease there than anywhere else, and [for him] it was a position of strength.'

In Brazil for the annual song festival, Françoise continued to agonise over Jacques' feelings for her. 'I felt fundamentally destabilised', she said. Whereupon Lena advised her to consult a medium (person claiming to be in contact with the spirits of the dead and to communicate between the dead and the living[2]), who informed her that she and Jacques had been 'in a relationship in a past life'!

On her return from Brazil, Françoise made an entire album, 'with Tuca on guitar and Guy Pedersen, an excellent [French] jazz musician, on stand-up bass. Also, the decision was made 'to add strings to most of the pieces [they] had recorded'. Finally, Tuca 'asked Raymond Donnez [French pianist, composer, arranger, and conductor] to write and direct what [they] had dreamed up together'.

French violinist, composer, and singer, Catherine Lara suggested that the Paris Orchestra be asked 'to perform Tuca and Raymond Donnez's string compositions. The results surpassed my expectations', said Françoise. 'I have never been as proud of one of my records as I was of this one.' Françoise's 11th studio album, entitled *La Question*, was released in October 1971.

Françoise spent much time trying to analyse her feelings for Jacques, and his for her. 'Initially', she said 'the absence, infidelity, and evasiveness of the other person exacerbate the feelings you think you are feeling for him, or at least the need you have for him. During our too rare moments of intimacy, Jacques showed evidence of tenderness, sensitivity, possessiveness, and jealousy, which gave me the impression that I mattered as much to him as he did to me. Perhaps I was only seeing what I wanted to see.'

In other words, Françoise was beginning to realize that she had been in denial in respect of her relationship with Jacques. She was also aware that he was being unfaithful to her.

Press photographer Jean-Marie Périer, Françoise's former fiancé, observed that while she 'was alone at home in a very bad way', Jacques was 'having fun'. So Périer asked Jacques outright, 'And what about Françoise in all this'. 'I love her', he replied, but 'I don't want to be like everyone else: see no one but her at the beginning, then cheat on her at the end. It would be better to start with the end, and end with the beginning'. When Jean-Marie told Françoise this, her reaction was understandable. 'I felt short-changed', she said.

Françoise became introspective and sought reasons to blame herself for the impasse with Jacques. 'I became convinced that in so many situations, a person is never completely innocent of what happens to them'. As far as Jacques was concerned, she said 'I was unhappy and demanding. I would have run away just as fast if he had shown this kind of face to me. I also realized that what led me to putting up so meekly with his vacillation between goodwill and meanness revolved around my lack of self-confidence. This not only prompted me to be happy with little, but to give much more back in exchange ... as if to compensate for my alleged deficiencies in all domains.'

Referring to her period with the French record label and distribution company, *Sonopresse* (1970-1973) which, Françoise said, had 'started off so well thanks to the success of my albums *Soleil* ['Sun'] and *Comment te dire adieu?* ['How To Say Goodbye To You?'], it 'ended on a sour note with three albums that, although my best by far, remained little known'. Furthermore, her contract with *Sonopresse* was not renewed. Nevertheless, she said, 'I have always thought it is better to make beautiful albums that do not sell, than the opposite'.

As Françoise approached her 30th birthday, due to take place on 17 January 1974, she confessed that she 'was dying to have a child with Jacques'. However, he was lukewarm about the idea and 'listed the various qualms [misgivings] inspired by the responsibilities I was encouraging him to take on'. However, he did not say either 'yes or no'.

In October 1974, Françoise was told by her gynaecologist that she was pregnant. 'I felt this was the best day of my entire life', she said. However, although she knew that Jacques was at his home, 67 rue de Provence, with his musicians, she did not 'dare to tell him the good news', and it was only several days later when he telephoned her from Noumea in New Caledonia, she said, 'that I could inform him of my condition'. Looking back, said Françoise 'I must have been so inhibited and so unsure of myself, and so unsure of the man I loved, to be so incapable of knocking on his door, despite my need to share my happiness with him so that he could take me, if only for a second, in his arms.'

Françoise described French singer-songwriters, Véronique Sanson [who was also a record producer] and Michel Berger as having 'a more international dimension simply because their songs were as rhythmic as they were melodic, and because their airy, efficient, sensitive, and assertive productions were just as good as anything from the other side of the Channel or the Atlantic'. She now made an interesting observation in respect of the 'yé-yé' [style of pop music that emerged in the early 1960s] singers. They 'were for the most part from the working class, whereas the wave that followed came from the middle class'. That is, 'from an educated background, to which they owed a musical training the previous generation lacked'. This was not snobbery on Françoise's part, simply a statement of fact.

At Périer's instigation, Michel Berger and Véronique Sanson paid a visit to Françoise in her 'little apartment on the Île Saint-Louis'. The outcome was, she said, that Berger 'agreed to produce my next album and write two of its twelve songs'. He also 'took responsibility for finding the other ten immediately after'. The album was *Message Personnel* ('Personal Message', released November 1973).

When both Lena and Yuca returned to Brazil, and Périer 'went to live at Mick Jagger's house in Great Britain for a while, and Jacques was no more available for my pregnancy than he had been before it', said Françoise 'I was even lonelier than before'. Her gynaecologist advised her to have the baby at Paris's American Hospital. 'I should have asked Jacques to bring me [there], but it never occurred to me. He did not offer either; or if he did, it was without conviction, so it was my mother who came to get me'.

Did Françoise's millions of fans throughout the world know that their idol, this beautiful, charming, and talented young woman whom they adored and who was by now a superstar of the pop world, harboured a dark secret? English poet, Thomas Gray (1716–1771) in 'Elegy written in a Country Churchyard', wrote the following couplet:

> Full many a flower is born to blush unseen,
> And waste its sweetness on the desert air

And Françoise was, and is still, one of the most beautiful flowers of all. Surely, this could not be happening to her?

There is no doubt that, despite all, Françoise remained deeply in love with Jacques and strove to please him in every way she knew how. Yet, she was in despair over his ambivalent attitude towards her. The question is, how would the situation be resolved?

1. Quinonero, Frédéric, *Françoise Hardy : Un Long Chant d'amour*, p.172.
2. Stevenson, A., and Waite, M., *Concise Oxford English Dictionary*.

18
A New Arrival: Thomas Dutronc, 16 June 1973

Françoise and Jacques's son, Thomas, was born on 16 June 1973 at 8.09 a.m. in the American hospital in Neuilly-sur-Seine, 5 miles west of Paris. She was 'overjoyed' and all the more so 'because Jacques also seemed quite happy'.[1] However, when she returned home with her 'precious little bundle of joy', she was to find that 'nothing changed in [their] lifestyle', she said, 'which seemed even stranger now that there was a baby'. She added: Jacques 'still lived at his place and came to mine around three times a month. My mother took care of Thomas for me when I had obligations'.[2]

Said Quinonero, 'Willingly giving in to the media ritual, Françoise Hardy and Jacques Dutronc welcomed a TV crew in the baby's room. In front of the cameras, they behaved like an ordinary couple who lived under the same roof, even though it was not always so'.[3] However, said Françoise, 'Our relationship is like a game of hide-and-seek. The only thing that we really have in common is the child. That's huge'.[4]

'When asked if the birth of his child was going to change his lifestyle', Jacques replied no. 'He is the one entering our lives. We are not going to change everything for him. He is the one who has to get used to our life'.[5]

'From his very first months', said Quinonero, Thomas Dutronc spent all his holidays in Corsica. It is where he feels he grew up'.[6]

In early 1974, Françoise was in cheerful mood, 'buoyed by the success of her album *Message Personnel* (released November 1973).[7] Also, in late 1974, French astrologer Jean-Pierre Nicola invited Françoise to contribute to an astrological magazine which he was planning to launch.[8]

When Mireille Hartuck convinced Françoise that she 'should entrust Thomas' to the care of his paternal grandparents Pierre and

Madeleine Dutronc once a week, in order that she 'could arrange a night alone with Jacques', this 'new arrangement', she said 'did not find fortune with the concerned party [i.e. Jacques] and did not improve our relationship whatsoever. I should have expected this because I know full well that he dreads one-to-ones and flees them whenever possible. It seemed to me that Jacques was able to put up with his new life only because I took care of all the tasks of daily life and because Thomas's presence made it so he did not have to be alone with me.'[9]

The heartbreak that this must have caused to Françoise can scarcely be imagined!

At her mother Madeleine's suggestion, Françoise invited Jacques to come and live with her and the new baby. 'As my flat was now too small', she said, she asked Jacques 'if he wanted me to find a place for the three of us'.[10] 'I took my courage in both hands and took the plunge', she said. 'I need a larger apartment. Should I look for one for Thomas and me, or for the three of us?' Françoise finally prevailed, and after some procrastination, Jacques finally agreed.

In autumn 1974, Françoise went to view a property 13 rue Hallé, in Paris's 14th arrondissement. 'I immediately felt that this was the place of my dreams' she said. Jacques also liked it because it had a garden, something 'he had always dreamed of'.[11] This was a 'three-storey house with an atrium and a solarium', near Paris's Parc Montsouris. 'Separate bedrooms, separate floors, separate schedules. Couples must have a daily call sheet in order to avoid skirmishes', said Jacques, ominously![12]

Thomas's infancy, which should have been a blissful time for Françoise, was bittersweet. Périer had convinced Jacques of his potential as an actor, but Françoise had reservations. Acting 'required a great deal more discipline' than singing. 'The singer remains in charge of what he does, whereas to a certain extent the actor is an interchangeable pawn' who could be 'quickly replaced'.[13] Nonetheless, Jacques did star in several films.

The film *L'Important c'est d'aimer* ('That most important thing: love'), starring Jacques Dutronc and German-French actress Romy Schneider, and directed by Polish director Andrzej

Zulawski, was released on 12 February 1975. When members of the production crew informed Jacques, in Françoise's hearing, that Romy 'needed to fall in love' in real life, and that he was to be her 'devoted lover', said Françoise, 'I was turned inside out'. And when she heard rumours that Jacques and Romy were 'together', 'the sky came crashing down on [her]'.[14]

This time, instead of trying to justify Jacques's actions, which she usually did, Françoise decided to take action herself. She went to his apartment and waited outside. 'I was determined to break things off and was feeling unhappier than ever before in my life', she said.[15]

Jacques finally arrived home at 8 o'clock the following morning. However, said Françoise, when he saw her in the 'pitiable state of the deceived, weeping woman ... not a muscle on his face quivered, as if he found my presence on his landing at this hour of the morning completely natural. He invited me in, and I felt torn between the obligation to break things off and the devastating impression that I could not live without him'.[16]

When she 'talked of leaving him', said Françoise, Jacques 'only advised me to get a little sleep and when he joined me to do the same, showed me that I still turned him on. That was his way of telling me that nothing had changed'. Jacques told Françoise that the reason for his absence that night was because 'a work meeting had been held that evening at Romy's'. 'What game had he been playing with me?' Françoise asked herself.

'Many years later', said Françoise, Jacques 'said that he had never cheated on me .... I clearly got what he meant: what happened below the belt didn't count'.[17] In other words, for Jacques to have sexual intercourse with another woman was fine as long as he remained faithful to Françoise in his heart. She now began another episode of introspection. Speaking of herself she said, 'How can you believe you are so wonderful that you should be enough for him in all things at all times?'[18] But her mind was not at peace.

'One night when I was hitting bottom even harder than usual, I did something forbidden – at least in my opinion - I called his apartment at three in the morning.' Jacques answered the phone, but Françoise could hear the 'eminently recognisable voice of his famous partner asking him if he wanted her to leave'. This 'new blow' prompted Françoise to act 'against her nature', and she decided to 'respond favourably' to a 'great Italian artist' who had been making advances to her. This served to restore 'a little of the self-confidence I had lost', she said. She terminated the relationship 'very quickly', but felt ashamed, selfish, and guilty 'for not treating him [the Italian] fairly', even though he was a married man.[19]

In the late 1970s Jacques introduced Françoise to a 'call-girl' name Susi, who advised her to be more 'sexy' and this, Susi believed, would be 'the key to everything'. However, 'decking myself out in "chic undies" or showing more of myself when washing the pots and pans' said Françoise, 'would have made me feel as if I was in disguise, and their only effect would have been entirely comical'.[20] She could not pretend to be someone that she was not.

When Françoise described herself as having an 'androgynous morphology' (i.e. partly male, partly female[21]), this again was an example of her self-critical attitude. After all no one could have mistaken her figure, admired as it was by both sexes throughout the world, for that of a man![22]

With regard to Jacques, said Françoise, 'It is so hard to know how to behave when the other person's emotional distance makes you want to stick your tongue out'. However, she drew the line at telling lies, and 'anything remotely resembling manipulation'.[23]

One day, fed up with 'being treated like a part of the furniture and taking advantage of Thomas's absence', Françoise 'took the unprecedented step of spending the night at a hotel'. Jacques, however, was unconcerned. 'This completely uncharacteristic defection did not even trigger the mildest reaction', she said,[24] and her agony continued unabated: 'How many times have I felt an ugly twinge in my heart when I see the man of my life making no effort to please me, and even going about looking or acting his worst? I concluded from this that how I felt was the least of his worries and, even worse, that he was maintaining a shield of being untouchable as a barrier to my possible bursts of enthusiasm. And the same heartache returned when I saw him trying to look his best when he went out without me. Was he merely conforming to the rules of life and society or was he hoping to please someone else?'.[25]

'It took me years to realize', said Françoise, 'that Jacques had an alcohol problem', which he eventually admitted to her. An 'uncustomary nastiness' was one of the features that 'betrayed his excesses. But during all those years when she 'did not realize what was going on', she said, 'I stupidly blamed his animosity towards me on everything he did not like about me - things I did not like either'.[26]

It was 'common knowledge', said Françoise, that predisposing factors to alcoholism were 'inferiority complexes, difficulty in being outgoing' and in 'expressing what you deeply feel, anxiety, and angst'. Was Françoise correct in her 'diagnosis' or did Jacques drink simply because he had what she described as 'a pleasure-seeker's temperament'?[27]

Jacques took Françoise to the screening of the new film *Le Bon et les Méchants* ('The Good and the Bad, released 21 January 1976), set in 1930s Paris in which he played 'Jacques', the eponymous gangster who, when the Second World War broke out, joined the French Resistance. She regarded this as 'one of his best roles', and this was 'probably because in many ways it matches his own personality: natural, sassy [lively, bold, full of spirit, cheeky[28]], insolent, cynical, the soft-hearted thug'.[29]

Jacques had once remarked to Françoise 'that it is better to have two children than just one'. She was therefore 'thrilled' when, in 1978, she became pregnant once again. The joy was short-lived. She had a miscarriage. When she told Jacques the bad news over the telephone, he 'seemed pleased. He had always "seen" himself with one boy, not two'. Also, she said, he 'could not hide his relief at seeing me pull through it so well. As for herself, 'this loss did not affect me in any lasting way', she said, because she had been wondering 'where I would have found the strength to multiply by two the anxieties one constantly feels as a parent'.[30]

1. Hardy, Françoise, *The Despair of Monkeys and Other Trifles*, p.125.
2. Ibid, p.126.
3. Quinonero, Frédéric, *Françoise Hardy : Un Long Chant d'amour*, p.238.
4. *Libération*, 29 April 2000, in Quinonero, Frédéric, *Françoise Hardy : Un Long Chant d'amour*, p.303.
5. Journal Télévisé, INA, in Quinonero, Frédéric, *Françoise Hardy : Un Long Chant d'amour*, pp.238-9.
6. *Version Femina*, 15 March 2012 in Q p.240.
7. Hardy, Françoise, *The Despair of Monkeys and Other Trifles*, op. cit., p.138.
8. Ibid, p.148
9. Ibid, p.155.
10. Leydier, Michel, *Jacques Dutronc*, in Quinonero, Frédéric, *Françoise Hardy : Un Long Chant d'amour*, p.239.
11. Hardy, Françoise, *The Despair of Monkeys and Other Trifles*, op. cit., pp.137-8.
12. *Libération*, 28 February 2000, in Quinonero, Frédéric, *Françoise Hardy : Un Long Chant d'amour*, p.239.
13. Hardy, Françoise, *The Despair of Monkeys and Other Trifles*, op. cit., p.127.
14. Ibid, pp.132-3.
15. Ibid, p.133.
16. Ibid, p.134.
17. Ibid, p.135.
18. Ibid, p.136.
19. Ibid, pp.136-7.
20. Ibid, p.156
21. Stevenson, A., and Waite, M., *Concise Oxford English Dictionary*.
22. Hardy, Françoise, *The Despair of Monkeys and Other Trifles*, op. cit., p.157.
23. Ibid, p.158.
24. Ibid, p.159.
25. Ibid, p.159.
26. Ibid, p.160.
27. Ibid, p.161.

28. Stevenson, A., and Waite, M., *Concise Oxford English Dictionary*.
29. Hardy, Françoise, *The Despair of Monkeys and Other Trifles*, op. cit., p.162.
30. Ibid, p.166.

19
Meanwhile, Life Goes On

When Lebanese-French composer Gabriel Yared asked Françoise to sing a song entitled *Jazzy Retro Satanas*, her response was, 'This kind of thing typically repulses me, as I am only interested in lyrics and melodies based on emotions - painful ones preferably - and I have nothing to give in songs of this nature'. Furthermore, she said, she did not hide from Gabriel her 'reservations about singing something so remote from my moods and attitude'.[1] Françoise did, however, record the song, and this, she said, proved to be her 'worst studio memory', so much so that 'I became increasingly convinced I should end my singing career once and for all'. Any artist who either has their work adulterated, whose work is not performed well, or who is required to perform a subject matter which is anathema to them, would have reacted in exactly the same way!

When Périer left for a twelve-year sojourn in the USA, said Françoise, a crucial source of support was removed. 'I now had to make my way without him', she said.[2]

Referring to *The Story of O*, an erotic novel by French author Anne Desclos (written under the pen name Pauline Réage and published in 1954), Françoise remarked that the novel 'goes far beyond the context of erotica as it primally deals with mad love and frustration'.[3] In fact, she chose 'Mad [i.e insane] Love' as the title both for her novel *L'Amour fou* (published by French publisher Albin Michel of Paris in 2012.) and for her 27th studio album (released 5 November 2012).

Once she 'had acquired a certain amount of fame', said Françoise, her father Pierre 'was unable to resist the human temptation to tell those around him that I was his daughter'. Her father also agreed to acknowledge Françoise and her sister

Michèle, thereby granting them 'rights to his inheritance'. However, this did not make up for the fact that in the past, her mother Madeleine had 'suffered greatly' from Pierre's 'miserliness'.[4]

When Françoise discovered that her father, now aged almost 80, was a homosexual, and that he was 'picking up young guys', this 'turned my stomach' she said. Pierre Dillard was finally 'bludgeoned by one of his "victims"' who was 'looking for money', as a result of which and he died on 6 February 1981.[5]

Meanwhile, what of Françoise and Jacques's son Thomas? Thomas started at a school in the neighbourhood at the age of five, and he soon became interested in dinosaurs. He subsequently attended the nearby Collège Sévigné, a French non-denominational private school founded in 1880. Here, as one of 'the most intelligent students', Thomas, like his mother, obtained his diploma at the age of sixteen.[6] 'I always felt that I was wanted', he said. 'It is fantastic to know that your mother loves you more than anything else'.[7]

Thomas enrolled in the University of Paris (the Sorbonne) 'and took courses in the visual arts, with cinema as an elective'.[8] And having pursued photography, he decided 'to devote himself to the guitar'.[9] When he left home, he went to live in 'a duplex [residence divided into 2 apartments] in the village of Saint-Paul' in the fashionable Marais district in Paris's 4th arrondissement'.[10]

Subsequently, Thomas purchased a house in Lumio, 'a village bathed in light' on Corsica's Balagne coast'. Here in Corsica, he said, 'Because they were famous, my parents rarely went to the beach. Essentially, my father would spend his time drinking and my mother reading books. Me, I was trying to salvage my mental health as best I could!'[11]

1. Hardy, Françoise, *The Despair of Monkeys and Other Trifles*, p.168.
2. Ibid, p.170.
3. Ibid, p.171.

4. Ibid, pp.175-6.
5. Ibid, p.177.
6. Ibid, p.174.
7. *Psychologies Magazine*, No. 283, March 2009, in Quinonero, Frédéric, *Françoise Hardy : Un Long Chant d'amour*, p.238.
8. Hardy, Françoise, *The Despair of Monkeys and Other Trifles*, p.245.
9. Ibid, p.246.
10. *La Libre Belgique*, 24 October 2008, in Quinonero, Frédéric, *Françoise Hardy : Un Long Chant d'amour*, p.303.
11. *Version Femina*, 15 March 2012 in Quinonero, Frédéric, *Françoise Hardy : Un Long Chant d'amour*, p.240.

20
The Wedding: 30 March 1981

Françoise and Jacques planned to get married in a civil ceremony to be held at the Town Hall, Monticello, Corsica. There were several reasons for this decision, as Françoise explained three and a half decades later, when she was interviewed on the privately-owned French radio station Europe 1. It was easier, because there were less formalities, and it was quicker. Also, a previous business partner of Françoise's had advised her that as she was due to have an operation, it would be better to marry in case something untoward happened. Her lawyer also agreed that this was the best course of action.

In early 1981, said Françoise, 'a small lump appeared near my right armpit'. The outcome was that she required a surgical operation, which was performed a few days before the wedding when a fibroadenoma was removed from her breast. She subsequently referred to 'the reassuring results of the fibroadenoma examination [i.e. biopsy]', an indication that her doctors believed this to be a benign tumour.[1]

The date was set for 30 March 1981, and the invited guests duly arrived. However, matters did not go well, and Françoise became upset for several reasons. The pair had an argument on the day of the wedding, on the steps of the Town Hall, when Jacques suddenly announced that he disliked the thought of getting married with his friends present as witnesses. This was despite the fact that they had all travelled there specially for the wedding. On this occasion, he was overruled by Françoise. During the party that followed, Jacques spent all his time with his friends, which meant that there was no social intercourse between his side of the family and hers.

After a day of celebrations, Françoise 'went up to bed around one in the morning hoping that [her] "new" husband would not be long in joining [her] there'. In fact, Jacques appeared at 3 a.m., exhausted after a prolonged bout of heavy drinking. He asked, 'in a whisper if [she] was happy', said Françoise, and then 'slept like a log', much to her disappointment.

Françoise was now obliged to return to Paris, where she was due to have her sutures removed, and she naturally assumed that Jacques, now her husband, would travel with her. She asked him 'several times if he had gotten his ticket, without ever getting an answer', and discovered that he had made other arrangements.

Their 'short stay on Corsica had been hopelessly platonic', said Françoise, and 'when we said out goodbyes at the airport I angrily shouted out, "This is definitely the last time I ever get married'. I did it without revealing how heavy my heart felt in the vague hope that he would enjoy my humour'.[2]

On what should have been the happiest day of Françoise's life, she was faced with a bizarre sequence of events which left her deeply upset, saddened, and disappointed, with the feeling that she had been thoroughly let down. To make matters worse, it would not be until five years later, in 1986, that Jacques finally purchased the couple's wedding rings. Whereupon Françoise wore hers on a chain around her neck. Said she, 'It is the only piece of jewellery that I really like, and I think I will be buried with it'.[3]

Meanwhile, between 1980 and 1984, said Françoise, Jacques 'made nine films in quick succession'.[4] As for herself, said Françoise, 'Like Jacques, I did all the television shows that were offered to me'.[5]

Françoise and their son Thomas visited the Portuguese island of Madeira where Jacques was starring in the (appropriately named!) film *Tricheurs* ('Cheaters'), directed by Iranian born Swiss film director and producer Barbet Schroeder. On the return journey, Françoise, Jacques, and Thomas stopped for a night in Lisbon. Knowing 'only too well' Jacques's 'apparent indifference to whether or not "they" share the same room or bed', said Françoise, she 'badgered him regularly to ensure he made the necessary hotel arrangements'.[6] Whether she was successful or not is unclear!

During the 1980s, said Françoise, she attended a course in psychology 'in the hope of finding a solution for my angst and discontent'.[7] She described a 'gap' that existed 'between me working too hard to make things work, and the other [Jacques], who was not working hard enough - I was doing the work of two!' This, she said, 'had caused me decades of suffering. With hindsight, I tell myself that I was much too demanding'.[8] Here, yet again, Françoise blamed herself for her unhappy marriage. But, she said, 'these were very special years! The feeling of love is an extraordinary motor, even if it is kept running by perpetual torment. Without it I would never have written a single song lyric'.[9] It is a fact that all too often, in whatever sphere, be it music or literature, creativity is born out of suffering.

In the late 1980s, Françoise expressed her disdain for politics. She said: '[it] interested me no more than it had twenty years earlier. I will simply mention the propensity of some socialists who like to play the prosecutor by brandishing ethical values (which they do not follow in their personal lives). The majority of leftist politicians seem to be as lacking in intellectual honesty as most right-wing politicians'.[10]

1. Hardy, Françoise, *The Despair of Monkeys and Other Trifles*, pp.180-1, 184.
2. Ibid, p.183.
3. Daho, Étienne, and Jérôme Soligny, *Françoise Hardy, Superstar et Ermite*, Éditions Grancher, 1986.
4. Hardy, Françoise, *The Despair of Monkeys and Other Trifles*, op. cit., p.194.
5. Ibid, p.199.
6. Ibid, pp.195-6.
7. Ibid, p.200.
8. Ibid, p.200.
9. Ibid, p.201.
10. Ibid, p.212.

Image from LOOK - titled Françoise Hardy.

*Photograph. Brooks, Charlotte, and Thomas R Koeniges, photographer.
Retrieved from the Library of Congress.*

Francoise Hardy in London, mid 1960s.
Everett Collection Inc / Alamy Stock Photo

Francoise pictured with her fiancé, the press photographer Jean Marie Perier, son of the famous actor Francois Perier.

Keystone Press / Alamy Stock Photo

"Francoise Hardy, french teenager, will be performing her song Love Goes Away at this years Eurovision Song Contest, representing Monaco. The 1963 contest is being staged at BBC TV Centre, London"
pictured 22nd March 1963.

Trinity Mirror / Mirrorpix / Alamy Stock Photo

French singer Françoise Hardy posing in her Paris apartment located Île Saint-Louis.
c.1970 Photo Michael Holtz
Photo 12 / Alamy Stock Phot

"French actress and singer Francoise Hardy, Germany 1970s"
United Archives GmbH / Alamy Stock Photo

French singer Thomas Dutronc (son of French singers Jacques Dutronc and Francoise Hardy) performs live with his band 'Thomas Dutronc et les Esprits Manouches' at the 'Cafe de la Danse' jazz joint in Paris, France, on October 14, 2006.

Photo by Nicolas Khayat/ABACAPRESS.COM
Abaca Press / Alamy Stock Photo

Musik aus Studio B, Musiksendung, Deutschland 1966, Gaststar: Francoise Hardy vor dem Auftritt in Hamburg

United Archives GmbH / Alamy Stock Photo

FRANCOISE HARDY, *French chanson singer and film actress in Germany, 1966.*
United Archives GmbH / Alamy Stock Photo

French singer Françoise Hardy, August 1971.

Photo Michael Holtz
Photo 12 / Alamy Stock Photo

French singer Françoise Hardy walking in a street near the apartment she just rented on the Île Saint-Louis. c.1970

Photo Michael Holtz
Photo 12 / Alamy Stock Photo

21
With Her Music, Triumph!

Françoise and French actor Benoît Allemane co-presented a regular talk show on Radio Monte Carlo (RMC), the theme of which was astrology. However, in late 1988, RMC failed to renew her contract. 'For the first time in twenty-five years', she said, 'I was free of any professional commitments'.[1]

Meanwhile, on 2 March 1991, French musician, singer-songwriter, author, film-maker and actor Serge Gainsbourg died, Françoise declared that 'his departure signalled the end not only of an entire era but also our youth'.[2]

In spring 1991, Françoise spent two weeks promoting her music in the Japanese capital Tokyo.

When Françoise was asked to contribute to a double album, entitled *Urgences*, whose profits were going to AIDS research, she obliged by recording the song *Même si ça fait mal* ('Even If It Hurts', lyrics by Françoise, music by French composer, guitarist and singer Alain Lubrano), which I thought was outstanding'. It was subsequently entitled *'Si ça fait mal'* (released 1993). The video recording of this song, she said, 'remains by far the one of which I am most proud'.[3]

When Françoise signed a contract with Virgin EMI Records in December 1994, she said, here 'I found all the professional and friendly support I needed'.[4] In 1995, she commenced recording her first Virgin album (*Le Danger*, released 22 April 1996) at the ICP (Inter Chemicals and Plastics) recording and mixing studio in avenue Émile de Beco, Brussels, Belgium. Here, said Françoise, she enjoyed 'solitary morning walks' in the nearby woods, finding that 'immersion in nature ... was a form of meditation'.[5]

Françoise was infuriated whenever her music was adulterated, for example, when the CD of *Revenge of the Flowers* (Music by

Lee Gorman; Lyrics in English by Malcolm McLaren; lyrics in French by Françoise Hardy) arrived by post, she discovered that 'the splendid rhythm over which I sang had been replaced by a vague disco rhythm in the poorest taste. It made me weep with rage'.[6]

Françoise described the duet *I'll be Seeing You* (lyrics by US lyricist Irving Kahal, music by US composer Sammy Fain), which she had performed with US musician, singer, and songwriter Iggy Pop in 1997, as 'one of the recordings of which I am most proud'.[7] Iggy 'shared many traits in common with Jacques', she said. Both were 'reserved, down to earth, instinctive, crafty, and with a taste for young, Eastern women - not excluding the occasional nympho'.[8] By now, Françoise was under no illusions whatsoever about her husband!

Françoise admitted to being naive when it came to the matter of trust. 'Like all people who do not know how to lie, I often believe whatever anyone tells me', she said.[9]

In March 2021, Françoise denied that Jacques was in any way her mentor, when it came to her music. In fact, she found the suggestion 'quite ridiculous'![10]

1. Hardy, Françoise, *The Despair of Monkeys and Other Trifles*, p.226.
2. Ibid, p.222.
3. Ibid, pp.228-9.
4. Ibid, p.248.
5. Ibid, p.254.
6. Ibid, p.256.
7. Ibid, p.267.
8. Ibid, p.266.
9. Ibid, p.285.
10. Locoge, Benjamin, 'Françoise Hardy: Mes chansons m'aidaient à supporter mes douleurs' ['My Songs Helped me to Endure My Pains'], *Paris Match*, 23 March 2021.

22
With Jacques, Disaster! Spiritualism: Health Problems Loom

As a child, Françoise had been devoted to her mother. Now, however, tensions arose as a result of Madeleine's regular visits to the rue Hallé. 'She acted as if she was in her own home', said Françoise, and furthermore, she 'began increasingly displaying the scorn Jacques inspired in her'.[1] Clearly, Madeleine believed that her daughter would not find lasting happiness with Jacques.

'Once her hackles were up, she transformed into a terrifying, hard, impervious person that I detested'.[2] But Françoise was extremely reluctant to send her 'back to the emotional desert from which she came. She had no friends or relatives except for my entourage and me'.

Up until now, Madeleine, as a qualified bookkeeper, had been helping Françoise with her accounts. She now declared that 'she wanted nothing more to do with them or anything else connected with [her]', as she did not trust Jacques.[3] Nevertheless, Thomas continued to visit his grandmother regularly in Montmartre.[4]

In 1990, said Françoise, Jacques was engaged in the filming of *Van Gogh*, directed by French film director, screenwriter, and actor Maurice Pialat, in which he played the part of the eponymous hero.

One night in 1991, said Françoise, when Jacques had reached a low ebb, she revealed to him 'what had happened to [her] three years earlier', i.e. that she had fallen in love, even though the affair was brief and the relationship was platonic. She did not disclose the identity of her suitor. However, Jacques's 'violent reaction was completely unexpected - coming as it did from someone who had long given me the impression that I was part of the furniture. It was clear that he felt betrayed and deeply wounded. This was the evening on which he boasted that he had never deceived me. He explained that even if he spotted the slightest risk of falling in love with another woman, he took steps to avoid the danger. I told him that a person cannot decide to fall in love, and when you see that you have, it is too late, the damage has been done without your knowing, much less choosing.'[5]

'Both privately and publicly', said Françoise, Jacques 'now displayed a very embarrassing coolness towards me'. However, 'we did not cut our bridges because of it, nor have we ever cut them'.[6]

When Françoise's mother Madeleine was diagnosed with Amyotrophic Lateral Sclerosis, a progressive disease which causes paralysis, she 'telephoned me to find her a doctor who would be able to euthanize her. My mother and I have always been staunch advocates of euthanasia',[7] even though it was illegal in France at that time. 'The wall erected between us by our respective lack of understanding had become insurmountable and the power game she played did not help matters.'[8]

On the day of her mother's euthanasia in 1991, Françoise travelled to Montmartre and offered to be with her and present at the time of the injection. But Madeleine was 'absolutely aghast at the idea of my witnessing her death'. Françoise went to the town hall to collect the death certificate. She said: 'Jacques came with me of his own accord, and we waited together'. This was 'despite the deterioration of our relationship. Oddly, I felt neither sorrow nor grief, simply a huge feeling of relief', she said, both for her mother and for herself.[9]

Françoise did not go to Corsica in that year of 1991, nor again for several summers. 'My doomed love was too taxing, my relationship with Jacques had become impossible'. Meanwhile, she said, 'I hoped that by staying in Paris, the new object of my torment would come to join me there'. This was a reference to Thomas, who 'was very much in love with his delightful girlfriend'.[10] 'This did not happen. Deep down, I felt hugely guilty that I was a failure on every level. My only recourse was to hide away from prying eyes, as if I were a sick animal'.[11] Once again, instead of recognizing the problem as being Jacques's unwillingness to commit, Françoise turned in on herself.

On 29 December 1991, Jacques suddenly announced that his mother Madeleine had died. Françoise and Thomas attended the funeral, together with 'the entire Dutronc family'.[12]

Françoise 'became addicted to card readers [readers of tarot cards, used for fortune telling]', such as French singer, actress, and singing teacher Armande Altai, 'and the hopes they dangled in front of [her].' 'It perked me up and helped me wait for time to do its murderous work. I say murderous because first your feelings are fanned into flame by unrequited love, and then slowly but surely it extinguishes them. A love without any physical nourishment is like living entirely on dreams or imagination. Death by starvation puts an end to sufferings that you would not wish on your worst enemy'.[13]

Why did Françoise allow herself to be tormented so? Why could she not draw a line under her failed relationship with Jacques and move on?

In August 1992 Françoise learnt that Michel Berger had died, on the 2nd of that month.[14]

In August 1994 a letter arrived from Germany informing Françoise that her sister Michèle was suffering from paranoid schizophrenia.[15]

In December 1996, Françoise learned that Mireille Hartuck had died, on the 28th of that month.[16]

On 17 June 1997, Françoise met the Dalai Lama, the spiritual leader of Tibet. They discussed Ayurvedic medicine, a traditional Indian practice designed to cleanse the body.[17]

In autumn 1998, Françoise relocated to 'a charming little duplex in the 4th arrondissement. This, she said, would offer Jacques and I enough autonomy to give us the space to receive whoever we wished without disturbing each other'.[18] But far from being happy and content, said Françoise, 'I felt a deadly sense of dread rising through me'.[19]

When Françoise interviewed French author Michel Houellebecq for the astrology magazine *Astrologos*, she said, 'I was touched by the suffering and loneliness I saw inside him'.[20]

It was by chance that Françoise happened to see a performance by classical pianist and spiritualist Hélène Grimaud on her television set. 'I had no inkling then of the importance this veritable lightning bolt would have in my life', she said. Shortly afterwards, Françoise wrote a documentary piece about 'the beautiful Hélène' for the French TV channel Canal+, and the entire interview was subsequently published in *Paris Match*.[21] Great musicians, said Françoise, were 'actually performing the role of mediums, by seeking to attain the music's soul in order to pass it on to us'.[22]

By the year 2000, said Françoise, her relationship with Jacques had taken 'on the form of a singular friendship'. He confided to her that he was distressed, having experienced 'a sudden resurgence of passion' in respect of 'a woman who had made him suffer greatly' at some time in the past. They had dinner together at a restaurant, an experience, said Françoise, which 'had been all too rare to my liking', and Jacques told her of his hopes in relation to the new love in his life. Whereupon she pointed out to him 'his problem with commitment, but he had obviously not looked at the situation from this angle'.[23]

Nevertheless, said Jacques, 'I will never get divorced'. It was Françoise's opinion that, 'For good or ill, he was perhaps not ready to let go of the security that I represented'. Jacques 'tenderly took my hand' she said, 'like in the good old days, for which we both remained eternally nostalgic'. However, it was her opinion that Jacques's 'statement appeared driven less by a need to spare me than by his congenital difficulty in challenging certain things, a kind of resistance to change that is sometimes confused with faithfulness'.[24] Nevertheless, despite 'solitude, the passage of time, and habit', she said, 'each of us continued to embody the other's most beautiful notions of paradise lost'.[25] But perhaps the notions were more vivid in Françoise's mind than they were in Jacques's'.

When the current object of Jacques's desire responded negatively, said Françoise, 'deep down, I regretted it. I would far prefer to see him happy with someone else, at least more alive thanks to her, than extinguished with me. Our relationship had long since ceased being satisfying – so, much the better if he set off on a new adventure that would give him the zest he needed while forcing him to evolve. However, if he really wanted to renew his relationship with that woman', said Françoise, 'he would have to re-examine the way he had been relating to the opposite sex from top to bottom. But he did not listen to me'.[26] Several months later, Françoise learnt that Jacques had fallen in love with someone else, a woman 15 years his junior, 'whom he had met on a film shoot'. Her name was 'Sylvie D.' (Sylvie Duval).[27]

Meanwhile, when, on 11 September 2001, Françoise witnessed on television the destruction of the Twin Towers of the World Trade Center in New York City by terrorists, she 'could not help from crying'. Never afraid to voice her thoughts, she believed that Western governments 'bore a major part of the responsibility' for this, by 'constantly brandishing a theoretical superiority of the universal values they claim to represent, while endlessly pursuing policies that are scandalously amoral toward the world's other peoples, especially those of the Middle East'.[28]

In late 2003, Françoise, developed a sudden deafness, and subsequently her eye became inflamed. On 3 January 2004, her doctor informed her that a blood test showed that she had MALT (slow-growing Mucosa Associated Lymphoid Tissue) lymphoma. When she attended hospital for a full examination, Jacques accompanied her, 'and would be present throughout, with or without Sylvie D, whenever I felt the need'.[29]

Françoise was offered radiotherapy treatment, but she refused it, on account of possible side effects. Whereupon the doctors proposed 'a finely-tuned chemotherapy procedure'.[30] It was in these circumstances, she said, that she wrote the lyrics 'for a magnificent tune' composed by French composer, guitarist and singer Alain Lubrano and French songwriter and composer Pascale Daniel'. The song was entitled *Tant de belles choses* (released November 2004).[31]

Meanwhile, in late May 2004, Françoise learned that her sister Michèle had died in her Paris apartment.[32]

Françoise has described how, when she was not too tired and time permitted, she would walk in the Parc de Bagatelle, a botanical garden located in the heart of Paris's Bois de Boulogne. Her favourite tree, she said, was called the 'Despair of Monkeys' (*Araucaria araucana*, in English the 'Monkey Puzzle Tree'). This 'reminds me of men who have caused me despair. They, too, discourage people from getting too close by making themselves inaccessible or by casting thorns. Fragile as they were, how could they have done otherwise?'[33] This was a clear allusion to Jacques Dutronc, whom Françoise, rightly or wrongly, had always regarded as 'fragile'.

1. Hardy, Françoise, *The Despair of Monkeys and Other Trifles*, p.223.
2. Ibid, p.225.
3. Ibid, p.225.
4. Ibid, p.225.
5. Ibid, pp.230-1.
6. Ibid, p.232.
7. Ibid, pp.232-3.
8. Ibid, p.236.
9. Ibid, pp.238-9.
10. Ibid, p.239.
11. Ibid, p.239.
12. Ibid, p.239.
13. Ibid, p.240.
14. Ibid, p.243
15. Ibid, p.250.
16. Ibid, p.263.
17. Ibid, p.269.
18. Ibid, p.274.
19. Ibid, p.277.
20. Ibid, p.281.
21. Ibid, pp.285-6.

22. Ibid, p.287
23. Ibid, pp.290-1
24. Ibid, p.291.
25. Ibid, p.291
26. Ibid, p.291
27. Ibid, p.292
28. Ibid, pp.293-4.
29. Ibid, pp.298-9.
30. Ibid, p.299.
31. Ibid, p.300
32. Ibid, p.303
33. Ibid, p.311

23
What Françoise Longed For and what was On Offer

Said Hadi Kalafate of Françoise, 'She immediately idealised her relationship with Jacques, just as she had done with Jean-Marie [Périer]. But of course, she was disappointed, because Jean-Marie was always "here and there taking photos". Jacques, however, was always busy boozing it up and larking around with his mates, like some retarded teenager. He couldn't live without his mates. We used to go out almost every night, usually to Castel. There were girls all around us, like Zouzou. Françoise kept well away. Each to their sleepless nights'.[1]

'One day, Jacques told me something about Françoise which perfectly sums up the situation', Kalafate continued. 'I put her on a pedestal, and I rolled around in the mud at her feet'.[2]

As for Françoise, she said of Jacques, he 'belongs to the category of slightly disconnected men: there is what is below the belt, which does not matter one bit, and what is above. The person who manages to sustain the interest of this type of man is then put on a pedestal, from whence she is not brought down often enough'.[3]

In regard to her 'coping mechanism', Françoise declared: 'One day, a Swiss journalist gave me a recording called "Omnia Pastor". Omnia is the pseudonym of a medium who transmitted the thought of Pastor, nickname of a non-incarnate spiritual guide. I immediately adhered to his luminous answers.'[4]

Of Pastor she said: 'Some of the thoughts helped me a lot. For example, he says that we must not believe that every problem has a solution. Faced with a problem, you have to know how to look at it objectively and let it go if you can't solve it.'[5] The problem was that Françoise was unable to 'let go'!

Françoise said of Jacques, 'You cannot talk to him. Everything stems from the unspoken'.[6] Lanzmann, said of Jacques that he 'immediately defused every conversation which appeared to be too serious'.[7] Finally, said Kalafate, in Jacques's flat 'it was party time every night'.[8] By contrast, said Zouzou, 'Françoise was not a party animal. She wasn't one for the nightlife'.[9]

1. Interview with the author (Quinonero), July 2016, in Quinonero, Frédéric, *Françoise Hardy : Un Long Chant d'amour*, p.202.
2. Interview with the author (Quinonero), July 2016, in Quinonero, Frédéric, *Françoise Hardy : Un Long Chant d'amour*, p.204.
3. *Le Parisien*, 9 October 2008, in Quinonero, Frédéric, *Françoise Hardy : Un Long Chant d'amour*, p.205.
4. Révillion, Bertrand, 'Françoise Hardy: "A medium paved the way for me"', psychologies.com, 10 Apr 2013.
5. Hardy, Françoise, *Nouvelles Clés* (2nd extract), 19 March 2010.
6. *Le Nouvel Observateur*, 9 October 2012.
7. Jacques Lanzmann, Jacques, Le Voleur de hasards, J. C. Lattès, 1992, Ref 2, p.204, in Quinonero, Frédéric, *Françoise Hardy : Un Long Chant d'amour*, p.204.
8. Interview with the author (Quinonero), July 2016.
9. Interview with the author (Quinonero), June 2016, in Quinonero, Frédéric, *Françoise Hardy : Un Long Chant d'amour*, p.202.

24
Françoise and Jacques: An Avoidant Relationship

Not for a week, not for a month, not for a year, but for *decades*, Françoise soldiered on, resigned to gather up the proverbial crumbs from Jacques's table; living on a diet virtually devoid of the emotional warmth that one expects in a loving and romantic relationship.

Françoise has used many adjectives to describe Jacques, not all of them complimentary, but the word 'unkind' (in French 'méchant'), is not one of them, for she did not regard him as being deliberately unkind to her. His avoidance of her, she believed, was *her* fault, it was due to her clinginess and shortcomings, and to the fact that she demanded too much of the relationship.

She therefore looked inwardly, whereas if she had taken one step back, or had the kind of expert marital and relationship guidance been available to her then, that is available today, she would have quickly realized that Jacques's avoidant behaviour towards her had its roots in his own particular psychological make up. But for her, this realization was impossible and as a result, she was perpetually in denial, always giving Jacques the benefit of the doubt, and using 'confirmation bias' (the tendency to search for, interpret, favour, and recall information in a way that confirms or supports one's prior beliefs or values[1]) to make sense of the situation. And all the time, Françoise was working hard at her musical compositions and performances, travelling all over the world to fulfil her numerous engagements, which often entailed spending many lonely nights in faraway hotel rooms, and latterly bringing up her son Thomas.

The question, therefore, is as follows: what was the nature of the almost superhuman force that attracted her to Jacques, like iron filings to a magnet?

Jacques was extremely handsome, yes, and in terms of style he was the epitome of French 'chic' (elegantly and stylishly fashionable[2]). Furthermore, he and Françoise had a common interest in music, both being musicians, composers, and singers. Also, said Françoise 'the few men I was attracted to were both musicians and of an ambiguous nature'.[3] But whereas Jacques was most at home 'living it up' in the company of his male friends, Françoise was of a more solitary nature and quite content, for example, to immerse herself in books, including those of the great writers of today and yesterday, or go for walks in the beautiful French countryside.

A person may fall in love with another literally at first sight, or the realization may be more gradual, as was evidently the case with Françoise and Jacques. One's eyes light on a person, who may be alone or in a group of other people. The image of that particular person, the beloved-to-be, imprints itself on the mind to a greater extent than that of his or her companions. The reason for this is not known for, as Irish writer, Margaret Wolfe Hungerford stated in 1878, 'Beauty is in the eye of the beholder'.[4]

In respect of Françoise, Jacques's face and physique, colour of hair and eyes, texture of skin, facial expression, the way in which he deported himself, the way he moved, his charming mannerisms, and his masculinity may all have been factors in determining that this was the person whom she found attractive above all others. Also, his attire, style of dress, and elegance may have impressed the youthful Françoise.

In addition to purely visual stimuli, other senses are also involved when it comes to falling in love. The object of desire's scent (whether natural or out of a bottle!); the timbre of their voice, and in respect of Jacques, the music that he composed and the manner in which he played and sang – all this may be part of 'the mix'.

Jacques could be tender, caring, and supportive, when he chose to be, qualities which would have appealed to Françoise enormously, for she too had her vulnerabilities. On the other hand, he was renowned for his non-conformity, rebelliousness, and insolence, characteristics which she may also have found fascinating, exciting, and alluring! Finally, the raw and unadulterated sex appeal, for which Jacques was also renowned, may have been a powerful factor!

It is a curious fact that a person only realizes that he or she is in love when it is too late! It has already happened, either at first sight, or in the course of an acquaintance. That person becomes lovestruck before he or she has even had time to consider the matter consciously, for everything has happened in the subconscious.

As time goes by and the couple see more and more of each other, love may deepen and if so, other factors come into play which serve to stimulate their wishes to be together; make a home together; share common interests; face adversity together; and have children.

However, Françoise and Jacques's relationship was problematical, at any rate from her point of view, over the course of many decades. At the heart of this was the discrepancy between what she desired and what he was able to provide in the way of affection, companionship, and commitment. This was not necessarily a matter of fault on either side. This is not a blame game.

Françoise appears to have had no idea as to why Jacques was forever keeping her at arms' length. She failed to understand the reasons for his avoidant behaviour, and it is possible that Jacques did not understand them himself! The question arises, was Jacques only avoidant towards Françoise, or was he avoidant towards everybody he met?

Certainly, there were men whom Jacques disliked, but he was definitely not avoidant towards his close circle of male friends. However, was he avoidant to women, especially to those potential female partners who desired commitment? Françoise's remark to him that 'he would have to re-examine the way he had been relating to the opposite sex from top to bottom' indicates that yes, he was.

The question is, why did Françoise persevere with this 'avoidant' relationship?

1. 'Confirmation Bias', *Wikipedia*.
2. Stevenson, A., and Waite, M., *Concise Oxford English Dictionary*.
3. *Les Inrockuptibles*, No. 22, April 1990.
4. Margaret Wolfe Hungerford, *Molly Bawn*, (1878) 'Beauty is in the eye of the beholder'.

25
'Commitment Avoidancy' and its Origins

Clearly, it would be inaccurate to describe Jacques Dutronc as being 'avoidant' – one who contrives not to meet other people. After all, Jacques had numerous close male friends. Neither did he avoid Françoise all of the time. However, he was unable to commit to their relationship in the same way that she was, and therefore, the term 'commitment avoidant' is more appropriate in respect of their long and problematical relationship.

German marriage counsellor Diana Boettcher described how people who suffer from commitment anxiety (or 'commitment phobia') perceive emotional and physical closeness 'as a threat. Instead of seeking a serious relationship after the initial infatuation, they usually distance themselves'.

<u>The origins of Commitment Avoidancy</u> (Author's comments in italics)

Said Boettcher, 'fear of commitment originates in early childhood, often in the first two years of life. It is often caused by a dysfunctional relationship with the mother, the father, or both parents'. And she cites having an 'overprotected childhood' as a possible factor in the person's subsequent unwillingness to commit.

It was certainly the case, that Jacques's parents, and especially his mother, were extremely indulgent towards him.

As regards fear of commitment, said Boettcher, its origin 'can be found in the past. Negative experiences such as disappointments, injuries or traumas that have not been properly dealt with can be the reason for relationship phobia. In many cases there was a very painful separation in the past, which damaged the trust. Then it's hard to commit again. The fear of having to experience such pain again is greater than the longing for closeness or love.'

By all accounts, Jacques had loving and supportive parents. However, he described an event which may have scarred him deeply, despite him having dismissed it with some bravado. That was when he was summarily expelled from school, by a female teacher.

'A lack of self-confidence and a negative self-image can also cause commitment anxiety', Boettcher continued. 'If you do not consider yourself lovable, you cannot imagine that someone else does.'

Françoise was highly critical of herself vis-à-vis Jacques.

The outcome of 'Commitment Avoidancy'

'When things get serious after several dates', said Boettcher, avoidant partners 'distance themselves and are out of reach for a while.'

This was certainly the case, over and over again, in respect of Jacques, to Françoise's intense disappointment and dismay.

'People with a fear of commitment are rather unreliable and, for example, often cancel appointments at short notice.'[1]

Françoise experienced this with Jacques on numerous occasions.

In June 2019 an article entitled 'Avoidant Personality' was published on the website GoodTherapy. It described how the 'Avoidant' 'may constantly worry about saying something wrong or embarrassing themselves. This worry leads them to withdraw. Since individuals with avoidant personality are sensitive to criticism, they may be more easily hurt by others.'[2]

Françoise often complained that Jacques remained silent, in circumstances when she was desperate for some kind of response.

In 2020, an article entitled 'Sexual Anorexia, Love Avoidants, and Relationship Cycles' was published on the website Carewell. It stated that 'Love avoidants are afraid of getting hurt. It may appear that they are aloof, unemotional, and cold, but beneath the surface their emotions are quite intense. Somewhere in their lives they have learned to numb their emotions.'

Françoise frequently found Jacques to be lacking in emotion.

'Often love avoidants attract anxious or ambivalent partners who pursue them in order to get their emotional needs met and the anxious-avoidant cycle of attachment ensues.'

Françoise would fit into the 'anxious' category, and the term 'anxious-avoidant cycle' is most appropriate to describe her relationship with Jacques.

'Love avoidants can say they really want a relationship and mean it, but because of deeper unresolved hurts, it does not play out that way in real life. They may marry and have a family but keep a certain distance that leaves spouses feeling bereft and lonely.'

One has only to read Françoise's book The Despair of Monkeys and Other Trifles to know that this is true.

'They may also have sexual anorexia because sex produces intimacy, feelings that are uncomfortable for them. If they get close, they could be abandoned, feel loss and get hurt and the hurt would be overwhelming.'

It is quite possible that Jacques felt this way in respect not only of Françoise, but of all potential female partners.[3]

On 9 October 2019, an article entitled 'Avoidant Attachment in Marriage' was published on the OnlyYouForever website. It described how the 'Avoidant' 'may behave in ways that seem like they are intentionally doing things to hurt you, and it is easy to take personally. But in most cases, there is no intent to harm or be difficult in the marriage.'

Although Jacques's avoidance caused Françoise much sorrow and despair, she evidently did not believe that he was deliberately trying to hurt her.

'The default posture of an avoidantly attached person is to not depend on others.' This 'may be because they are distrustful of close relationships or are afraid of relying on anyone else. It may also be because they do not want to experience the pain of rejection'.

'They may avoid being close enough to receive support from another' because they do not wish to be pressurised into having to 'offer support in return and have their efforts rejected. This may be because there have been times when they have depended on someone else, and it had led to disappointment. They may consider that to need someone else is to show weakness.'

In respect of women, Jacques himself admitted that he found them 'capricious' (given to sudden and unaccountable changes in mood and behaviour'[4]).[5]

Jacques evidently did not have a prolonged relation with any woman during his lifetime, which suggests that the desire to avoid commitment was deeply ingrained in his psyche. So why, when he entered into relationships with other women, did he not cut off entirely from Françoise? Possibly because she represented constancy and stability, someone to fall back on for emotional support, someone who provided a structure, albeit remote, to his life in that she was his wife and the mother of their son Thomas.

1. Boettcher, Diana, 'Commitment Anxiety: The Fear of Closeness', Couples Therapy Berlin, 8 September 2018, online.
2. 'Avoidant Personality', GoodTherapy, 11 June 2019, online.
3. 'Sexual Anorexia, Love Avoidants, and Relationship Cycles', Carewell, 2020, online.
4. Stevenson, A., and Waite, M., *Concise Oxford English Dictionary*.
5. 'Avoidant Attachment in Marriage', OnlyYouForever, 9 October 2019, online.

26
What If?

What if Françoise, who was on the wrong end of avoidant relationship, had received the type of expert counselling that is available today? According to US Neuroscientist Amir Levine and US psychologist Rachel S. F. Heller, the advice to her and to others like her would be as follows: your 'attachment needs' are 'legitimate'. You 'shouldn't feel bad for depending on the person you are closest to - it is part of your genetic makeup. A relationship, from an attachment perspective, should make you feel more self-confident and give you peace of mind. If it doesn't, this is a wake-up call!'; finally, 'above all, remain true to your authentic self'.[1]

---

[1] Levine, Amir, and Rachel S. F. Heller, *Attached*, p.272.

27
Françoise's Incredible Perseverance!

Based upon what Françoise has said and written, it is clear that what she always wanted was a loving and compatible partner with whom to share her life. And when she fell in love with Jacques Dutronc, which she undoubtedly did, she must have believed that she had discovered that partner. But unfortunately, life was not that simple!

When we fall in love, the object of our desire becomes a delight to our eyes, a joy to our ears, and a pleasure to all of our other senses. And it is common experience that when that magical moment of falling in love occurs, certain physiologically driven events may occur over which we have no control. We may blush; experience palpitations or a tight feeling in the pit of the stomach or a dry mouth; feel rooted to the spot; be at a loss for words. Our palms may become clammy, and our pupils may dilate. As to why we fall in love with a certain person, and not with another remains a mystery.

The insightful Françoise hinted that the decision to fall in love is not a conscious one, when she wrote of how 'the unconscious directs us towards individuals whose flaws are exactly symmetrical to our own, and who possess the very pieces that are missing from the puzzle of our personality, just like we possess the ones they lack'. This, she said, was 'definitely a very odd mystery'.[1]

The above changes, described above, of which anyone who has ever been in love will be aware, are the result of stimulation of the autonomic (i.e. automatic, or subconscious) nervous system (ANS), resulting in adrenaline being released from nerve endings. The effect is virtually instantaneous.

The ANS also stimulates certain glands to produce surges of powerful hormones, in particular adrenaline and oxytocin from the adrenal glands. Oxytocin the so-called 'love hormone', induces feelings of euphoria, which we now associate with being in the presence of our beloved.

But this is only the beginning. Further contact with our newly beloved causes a further release of such hormones, and if the relationship progresses to sexual intercourse, this results in ecstasy, as a result of great hormonal surges, which in turn leads to a strengthening of the hormonally induced bonding. In this way, we become addicted to our partners!

In 1988, said Françoise, 'the last thing I ever expected happened to me. During a professional trip abroad, I fell in love at first sight with a particularly brilliant and ambiguous man'. But, she continued, 'there could be no other love for me except the one already in my life. I thank heaven today for not granting my daily prayers to physically experience the passion consuming me. In a certain way, I was a prisoner of the prominence of my relationship with Jacques and all it meant'.[2]

Finally, if offspring result from the union of the couple, then such bonding helps to ensure that the parents stay together and provide a firm foundation of care in which the children can be successfully nurtured until such a time when *they in turn* can go out into the world, find a mate, and procreate. It is all part of nature's cunning plan, designed to ensure the continuity of the human race.

So, what say do we have in the matter when it comes to falling in love? The answer, strange as it may seem, is none! The truth is that the subconscious effectively hijacks our minds, and yet we may be misguided enough to believe that it is *we* who control our own destinies!

Was there an element of masochism (the enjoyment of an activity that appears to be painful or tedious[3]) on Françoise's part? Definitely not. In no way did she enjoy what can only be described as an apology for a marriage!

1. Hardy, Françoise, *The Despair of Monkeys and Other Trifles*, p.217.
2. Ibid, pp.215-6

3. Soanes, Catherine and Angus Stevenson (Editors), *Oxford Dictionary of English*.

28
How Easy it is to Fall in Love with the Wrong Person!

The subconscious operates, in this context, purely to encourage reproduction, and thereby the continuation of the species. In other respects, it is seemingly quite indifferent to our fate. It is no wonder then, that for those such as Françoise, who seek a relationship which is based on more than sex – i.e. one which is caring and loving, with shared values and common interests -, matters so often go awry.

When the subconscious decides who we are to fall in love with, it does so on the basis of our initial sensory experience of that person: voice, physique, movement, scent, touch, etc. And the whole phenomenon occurs before we have time to get to know that person's character, past life, interests, values, sense of morality. Instead, the subconscious mind makes the decision for us, a decision which, in the case of love at first sight, is based on the flimsiest of evidence – for example a glimpse of a physique which looks so attractive that it instantly 'blows the mind'. And in a split second, that person has been identified as the 'object' of our desire. As for reasoning, rational thought, and having the time to make a considered judgment, this simply does not enter into it.

Before we know it, and because of the effect of powerful 'love hormones on our systems, we are now in thrall to the newly identified beloved, and blind to his or her shortcomings or unsuitability, if they exist. To put it bluntly, we may mistake the ecstasy and euphoria produced by the release of oxytocin with love! How likely it is, therefore, that our subconscious had made the wrong decision, and in doing so, has condemned us to disappointment, frustration, and misery! This was evidently the case with Françoise. This is not to imply that there was anything intrinsically wrong with Jacques. It is simply a matter of incompatibility.

A photograph exists of Françoise and Jacques in their early 20s, sitting by a swimming pool as he plays the guitar, and she looks on adoringly. Another shows them standing in a doorway, she laughing uproariously, as they share a joke. In a third, they are in the mountains, and as he strokes her cheek with his forefinger, one may almost imagine Françoise purring like a cat who has got the cream! By this time, of course, the chain reaction has occurred, definitely for her, if not to the same extent for him. The autonomic nervous system has kicked in, triggered the release of love hormones, and in so doing has determined that subsequently, whenever the two have contact of any kind, the cascade of love hormones would be released again, causing a bond between herself and Jacques which she could not break, even if reason told her that it would be in her best interests to do so!

It is entirely understandable that Françoise fell in love with Jacques. After all, he is devastatingly handsome, debonair, and charming and, like herself, talented, musical, and creative.

Can lessons be learned?

In an ideal world, before entering into a possible relationship, a person might be wise first to attempt to establish a good rapport with his or her potential partner; become friends; identify what the two have in common; see if they care about the same things; more importantly, see if they truly care about each other; in short, see if they share that vital ingredient, 'empathy'. By laying such groundwork, the chances of a long lasting and meaningful relationship would be greatly enhanced.

However, nature has decreed otherwise; that it is the subconscious, rather than the logical, rational mind which identifies our future partner for us, and as often as not, it gets it wrong and makes fools of us, a fact which we may only discover when it is too late, as Françoise learned to her cost!

29
Jacques Expresses Remorse

In 2003 Jacques stated that his 'feelings for Françoise' had changed. 'We have matured. Now that I understand everything she went through, I regret what I may have done. It is sincere but it comes too late. I was like that and that is what I did. For me, Françoise was the icing on the cake, next to having a laugh and drinking with my mates'.[1]

In regard to his affair with Romy Schneider, Jacques had this to say: 'I behaved badly. I got carried away and had an affair with her. The attraction was there. But I did not respect her. She had such power that you had to be sturdy in her presence. I was caught in something I could not control. I was messing around, like I did in the film. In front of such strength, you feel destabilised. And I am no Mother Teresa.'

'I was not very honest; at the end of the day, Françoise is Françoise, and I was not going to leave her for Romy Schneider. Romy was a wounded woman and whilst making that film, I wounded another one, mine.'[2]

1. *Télémoustique* (Belgium), No. 4046, 13 August 2003, in Quinonero, Frédéric, *Françoise Hardy : Un Long Chant d'amour*, pp.303-4.
2. *Vanity Fair*, 22 January 2014, in Quinonero, Frédéric, *Françoise Hardy : Un Long Chant d'amour*, pp.247-8.

30
Françoise's Coping Mechanisms: How She Made Sense of the Long Separations that were Imposed Upon Her

On the positive side, Françoise stated that the happiest times of her life were the times that she had spent with Jacques. However, even after their marriage and at his instigation she was obliged to endure weeks and months of separation from the man she loved, and this in the knowledge that he was conducting affairs with other women. However, even though this can only be described as a miserable apology for a marriage, it was one from which she was either unwilling or unable to escape.

Those who remember the youthful, joyful, vivacious Françoise with that wonderful smile and quizzical expression will be astonished and dismayed that she could have come to this. So, how on earth did she cope with the disappointment, the loneliness, and the sense of betrayal?

<u>By living on memories</u>

Said Françoise, 'Love is a true nourishment and, when taken, it must leave you sufficiently full for any kind of separation to be possible. Any separation is painful, but what matters most is the happiness felt within the riches of the exchange, as well as the legacy left behind'.[1]

<u>By convincing herself that Jacques felt the same way as she did</u>

Said Françoise, 'The feeling that there was a kind of reciprocity hidden behind the absence is what helped me endure this very difficult relationship. This is why I never left.[2] His mystery, his elusiveness, his prolonged and frequent absences are the reasons I managed to remain in love with him for so long.[3]

By convincing herself that she could love for both of them

Said Françoise, 'To love the other for what he is rather than what one would want him to be requires a lot of discernment, generosity, side-stepping and detachment, she explained. When you reach this intensity of love, then you can "love for two". Whether the feelings are mutual or not is almost secondary. What matters is that the sentiments are authentic: there is no price to that, no limit.[4]

By being in denial

Said Levine and Heller, 'Many people who live in an avoidant-anxious trap have a hard time admitting to themselves and others that they are in a bad predicament. They talk themselves into believing that their partner's behaviour is not so bad'.[5] In other words, they are in denial.

Through spiritualism

Was it because of her belief in spiritualism that Françoise was able to convince herself that she was still close to Jacques, even when they were hundreds of miles apart – she in Paris, he in Corsica?

By compromise

Said Levine and Heller, such individuals may find 'a way to live with limited togetherness. They compromise. But make no mistake, the compromise is in no way mutual; it is in fact wholly one-sided. Instead of engaging in endless conflict that results in nothing but frustration and disappointment', they decide 'to change their expectations and reduce conflict to tolerable proportions'.[6]

1. *Nouvelles Clés*, in Quinonero, Frédéric, *Françoise Hardy : Un Long Chant d'amour*, p.298.
2. *Le Figaro*, 25 March 2010 in Quinonero, Frédéric, *Françoise Hardy : Un Long Chant d'amour*, p.277.
3. *Gala*, No. 1069, in Quinonero, Frédéric, *Françoise Hardy : Un Long Chant d'amour*, p.277.
4. Leydier, Michel, *Jacques Dutronc*, in Quinonero, Frédéric, *Françoise Hardy : Un Long Chant d'amour*, p.297.
5. Levine, Amir, and Rachel S. F. Heller, *Attached*, p.208.
6. Ibid, p.193.

31
Françoise Loses Patience: Letting go of the Dream and Summoning the Strength to Walk Away

Said Françoise in 1988, 'The concept of cohabitation also exists in love matters!'[1] This indicates that the notion of living together, a natural consequence of a loving partnership and something which Françoise longed for but was denied with Jacques, was always very much at the forefront of her mind. However, Jacques's 'mystery and elusiveness', she said, 'fuelled withdrawal symptoms which, to begin with, fanned the flames', but 'eventually extinguished them'.[2]

When the realization finally dawned on Françoise that her goal of a secure and meaningful attachment was never going to be reached, and she let go of the dream, what then?

For those such as Françoise, who seek attachment in an avoidant relationship, why is it so difficult to walk away? Why, asked Levine and Heller, was the process so 'excruciating. You might understand, rationally, that you should leave, but your emotional brain may not yet be ready to make that move. The emotional circuits that make up our attachment system evolved to discourage us from being alone'.

Nostalgia also plays a part. 'You will get overwhelmed by positive memories of the few good times you had together and forget the multitude of bad experiences. You'll recall how sweet he or she was to you the other day when you were distressed, and conveniently forgot that he or she was the one to hurt you in the first place.'[3]

In 2010, said Quinonero, Françoise described herself as having been 'a starry-eyed young girl', and as such, admitted that love had been her driven force, her creative energy. 'Otherwise', she said, 'I would never have written any songs. I was in love during my entire life. With the choir boy when I was younger, with comic strip characters later on. It really is virtual, but virtuality is also my strength.'

So, what was Françoise left with? One may sense her sadness as she wrote: 'Essentially, nowadays I live a mad passion by proxy! I would have loved to love like that. But it was not to be.[4] Fantasy is akin to dream, you need it to idealise, to escape reality. This has always been the case for me, even now that my personal life only exists inside my own head.'[5]

Finally, said Françoise of Jacques, 'All I want is for him to be well, with or without me'.[6]

1. *Paris Match*, No. 2037, 10 June 1988, in Quinonero, Frédéric, *Françoise Hardy : Un Long Chant d'amour*, p.277.
2. *Gala*, No. 1069, in Quinonero, Frédéric, *Françoise Hardy : Un Long Chant d'amour*, p.277.
3. Levine, Amir, and Rachel S. F. Heller, *Attached*, p.209.
4. *Télérama*, No. 3277, in Quinonero, Frédéric, *Françoise Hardy : Un Long Chant d'amour*, p.335.
5. *Le Parisien*, 31 March 2010, in Quinonero, Frédéric, *Françoise Hardy : Un Long Chant d'amour*, p.13.
6. Leydier, Michel, *Jacques Dutronc*, in Quinonero, Frédéric, *Françoise Hardy : Un Long Chant d'amour*, p.297.

32
Françoise Reveals Herself through her Own Lyrics

'My lyrics always have to do with my own life', said Françoise. 'I am not interested in writing a song which is not anchored in my experiences. Even if today my inspiration primarily comes from fantasy, it really is down to what I have lived.'[1]

Said Quinonero, 'through writing and song', Françoise 'tirelessly attempted to solve the mystery of the man/woman relationship, in the light of her own experiences'.[2]

In her book *Chansons sur toi et nous* ('Songs about You and Us'), published in 2021, Françoise lists her songs and explains the feelings that her lyrics reflected.

In fact, these lyrics which she composed over the course of almost 50 years, serve as a timeline and indicate her state of mind, hopes, dreams, joys and sorrows, aspirations, frustrations, and disappointments over this period. (Author's comments in italics.)

Excerpts are quoted from the following songs, to illustrate and summarize what Françoise intended to be their meaning:

<u>*J'ai jeté mon cœur*</u> ('I scattered my heart'): Released 1962, Françoise aged 18.

Françoise gives a false impression of self-confidence:

> I scattered my heart
> And I regret it
> Pleasure and happiness
> Often get mixed up
>
> I wanted to taste

> Everything at once
> And I forgot
> What it means
> To love truly

Françoise explained that she had so many 'self-esteem' issues at the time, that she tried to give the impression of being free and easy, adventurous, seductive, etc. Such bravado on her part, however, she said, could not be more removed from reality!

<u>Comme tant d'autres</u> ('Like So Many Others')
Released 1963, Françoise aged 19.

Françoise wonders, will I be a disappointment to my lover?

> You tell me that you love me
> Today, that's what you believe
> Is all this worth it?
> Others got bored before you

Françoise explained that these lyrics reflect a fear that the one you love, or think you love, idealises you, until he realizes what you are really like.

<u>J'aurais voulu</u> ('I Would Have Liked')
Released 1963, Françoise aged 19.

True beauty is more than skin deep.

> I found her too pretty
> I wanted to be her
> So that you long for me the way you longed for her

Françoise declared that she had always been fascinated by beauty, all the more so because she always thought she was devoid of any! She distinguished between superficial beauty, and the beauty of the soul within. She feared that any boy she was with would leave her for someone who was simply pretty on the outside.

À quoi ça sert? ('Why even try?')
Released 1968, Françoise aged 24.

Will Jacques reject me?

> Our two hearts are the same, they could turn out untrue
> We don't want to feel pain, yet maybe I love you
> Why even try to go away, why even try to hide away?
> I've got nothing to share, just this world my eyes see
> But if it's pain that fear, pain lets no-one go free
> Why even try to steal away, why even try to run away?
> Or to stay in your ivory tower
> Grow in peace like some secret flower alone - alone
> When the pain is a little less
> We forget there's no happiness alone - alone
> Share the stars in the sky, for they're all I can give
> Share these tears we must cry, if we love, if we live
> Why even try to stay alone, why even try to live alone?
> Share the stars in the sky for they're all I can give
> Share these tears we must cry, if we love, if we live
> Why even try to stay alone, why even try to live alone, alone?

Françoise said that this song was inspired by her confusion and uncertainty as to whether her secret attraction for Jacques Dutronc was reciprocated. The song was a vehicle for disclosing everything that she wished she could tell him face to face.

J'ai fait de lui un rêve ('I Had a Dream about Him')
Released 1968, Françoise aged 24.

Françoise admits to being under Jacques's spell!

> I had a dream about him
> Which prevents me from feeling
> Love or sorrow
> I no longer know how to suffer

Others come
And go
I do not want them to love me
My heart is in jail

Françoise stated that this song was written in 1967 when she could not get away from the spell that Jacques had unwittingly cast upon her.

<u>*Tu ressembles à tous ceux qui ont eu du chagrin*</u> ('You Resemble All Those Who Have Known Sorrow')
Released 1970, Françoise aged 26.

Françoise sees Jacques as a victim and longs to comfort him and say she loves him.

You resemble all those
Who have known sorrow
But the sorrow of others
Is of no interest to me
Because the eyes of others
Are not as blue as yours

And like all the people
Who have known sorrow
Your face often takes
A stern and faraway look
But the face of others
Is much less beautiful than yours

Because of a look, because of time of sorrow
I would like to say 'I love you' and I would like to say 'come to me'
But it is not possible to know whether one will do good or bad,
So, I say nothing

Françoise stated that this song was inspired by Jacques Dutronc, and by her feelings for him prior to their relationship commencing in 1967. She believed, rightly or wrongly, that behind his provoking, nonchalant, or even cruel façade, he was hiding an internal pain. And yet she was afraid to volunteer to console him, for fear of the reaction this might provoke.

<u>La Question</u> ('The Question')
Released 1971, Françoise aged 27.

Françoise feels she does not really know Jacques and she wonders why she remains in the relationship, such as it is.

> I do not know who you could be
> I do not know who you are hoping for
> I keep trying to get to know you
> And your silence disturbs my silence
>
> I do not know why I stay
> In a sea where I am drowning
> I do not know why I stay
> In an air which will stifle me

Françoise explained that she was inspired to write this song by the painful turn that her relationship with Jacques had taken.

Would Françoise's prayers ever be answered? Would Jacques ever respond to the coded, and sometimes more overt messages that she was attempting to convey to him through her songs, in the hope that he would hear them? Sadly for her, the fact that the plaintive song writing continued, indicates that the answer was no!

<u>Bruit de Fond</u> ('Background Noise')
Released 1972, Françoise aged 28.

Françoise had reached an impasse in attempting to communicate with Jacques

> And I talk, and I talk
> But when it is his turn

Either he remains silent
Or he answers the wrong question

He is my stone wall
And I am his background noise

These lyrics signal a fairly obvious chasm between Françoise and Jacques.

<u>Ce Soir</u> ('This Evening')
Released 1974, Françoise aged 30.

Françoise implies that she has a date, but she is full of apprehension.

Tonight there is someone
Who is taking me out to dinner
To primp myself a little
I am going to put on some make-up

I will dare do nothing
I will dare do nothing
I will be ill at ease

Françoise admitted that she wrote these lyrics in order to make Jacques jealous.

<u>Je n'aime pas ce qu'il dit</u> ('I Don't Like What He Is Saying')
Released 1974, Françoise aged 30.

Françoise tries to interpret Jacques's feelings.

He says she means a lot to him
But he is not faithful
And he is sure of nothing
Other than time goes by
That his fleeting affairs
Will make his day nicer

        And that they distance him from her
        Whilst bringing him closer to her

Françoise believes that her lyrics express Jacques's vision of their relationship, and she thinks she is quite near the mark!

<u>Partir quand même</u> ('To Leave, No Matter What')
Released 1988, Françoise aged 44.

The possibility of leaving Jacques has evidently occurred to Françoise.

        Disappearing
        From before his eyes
        No longer giving any sign

        Before it is too late
        To rewind
        Before it is too late
        To avoid the war
        Before saying 'I love you'
        Knowing how to leave, in spite of everything…

Françoise explained that this song was inspired by the problem Jacques seemed to be having with the idea of commitment.

<u>En résumé, en conclusion</u> ('To Sum Up, to Conclude')
Released 1989, Françoise aged 45.

Françoise was full of foreboding.

        He does not talk a lot
        He smiles and that's it
        -and that's too much-
        I can foresee
        Very slippery slopes

        He surrounds himself with an igloo

I am wondering what he is playing at
-if he is playing-
His disconcerting looks
Attract me like a magnet

Who can tell me
The purpose of memory
If I cannot
Already escape
The mousetrap
About to be set?

To sum up
It is going to hurt
I am going to dive
This bloke is going to make me suffer
An everlasting ordeal

Françoise realized that, because of her love for Jacques, she was trapped in a relationship that will cause her endless pain.

<u>L'Obscur Objet</u> ('That Obscure Object')
Released 1996, Françoise aged 52.

Françoise longed for Jacques to change.

You are the clear object
Of the darkest desires
That you discourage
In your strange way

You are, to be clear, the object
Of the darkest thoughts
Why not, for once,
Change wavelength?

You are the ideal target
You, the heart in winter,

> You who hurt so much
> Whilst trying not to hurt…

Françoise could not understand why Jacques was so discouraging, although he did not mean to hurt her, even though he was hurting himself.

<u>Les Pas</u> ('The Steps')
Released 2010, Françoise aged 66.

Françoise was seriously ill, and this is reflected in her lyrics.

> A slightly special
> Perfume floats around,
> Subtle and heady
> Nothing abnormal
> It is just a bit painful
> To die in the spring
>
> Counting the hours
> Waiting for one's hour
> It is nearly time
> To feel the last blues

This song dates from 2009, Françoise having been diagnosed with lymphoma in January 2004.

<u>Rendez-vous dans une autre vie</u> ('Let's Meet in Another Life')
Released 2012, Françoise aged 68.

Françoise anticipates her death.

> Sorry if I leave on the sly
> And without warning
> Sorry for tonight, for yesterday also
> The play is over
>
> Let's meet later, in another life

Somewhere else or here
To love each other better and more than today
It is only a period of grace

And if we made a date
In order to respect
This strange pact
Maybe entering the narrow door
Would not be quite so sad?

Françoise dreams of meeting Jacques again in the afterlife. This would make the pain of being separated from him easier to bear, and perhaps they could make a better job of loving one another next time around!

<u>Personne d'autre</u> ('No One Else')
Released 2018, Françoise aged 74.

For Françoise there is no other love except Jacques.

A sign, like a call
A timeless air
Nobody other than you
To hear it

Your sky-coloured eyes
Something surreal
And me, staying here,
Waiting for you

The reference to 'sky-coloured eyes' is a giveaway that Françoise is referring to Jacques.

<u>Quel dommage</u> ('What a Shame')
Released 2018, Françoise aged 74.

The poignancy expressed by Françoise's lyrics, as she looks back regretfully on what might have been, is almost palpable.

I can hear the music
And I can see us again
So romantic
You as much as I

Where are the photos
Of those faces
So young, so beautiful?
Dear God, what a fall into the abyss!

So young, so beautiful
Dear God, what a shame!

<u>Trois petits tours</u> ('Three Little Turns')
Released 2018, Françoise aged 74.

Françoise bewails the enigmatic nature and elusiveness of Jacques. She realizes that she cannot force him to come to her, yet she believes, rightly or wrongly, that he too is in inner torment.

He is an enigmatic boy
A ferret which slips between your fingers
Did you see him come this way
And leave that way
Without stopping just one time?
Three little turns and off he goes

I do not know if he is nice
Sometimes he is almost cat-like
You never hear him arrive
But suddenly he is here
Smiling, not talking
Three little turns and off he goes

Alone in my bunker
I think I understand his absences
And I think I can hear his silences
His beating heart

> He sometimes is cynical
> Like a bear, he worries and scares others
> One must just not force things
> Not act like the strongest one
> One must let him come to you
> Three little turns and that's it
>
> Alone in my bunker
> I hear the call of his soul
> Like a pain, an alarm
> A plea from the heart
>
> I would like him to play me his music
> And to play mine to him also sometimes
> But never mind if he is not available
> All the impossible dreams
> Have given me the tune
> Three little turns and here you go
>
> Life, love, that's the way it is
> Three little turns and off they go…

Finally, Françoise accepts that her dream can never be realized.

For Françoise, writing such lyrics was a catharsis, as she herself admitted. She hoped that Jacques would hear the messages she sent him via her songs, and those songs helped her deal better with the pain, and she freed herself from that pain whilst she wrote and sang them.[3]

This, then, is the timeline of a beautiful and talented young lady who dreams of love and fulfilment, something which comes to her only fleetingly. And yet, by all accounts, Jacques did not pressure her in any way, apart from saying that he would never divorce her. Her choice, to be content with the meagre crumbs from his table, was hers alone.

1. *Ouest-France*, April 2010, in Quinonero, Frédéric, *Françoise Hardy : Un Long Chant d'amour*, p.328.
2. Quinonero, Frédéric, *Françoise Hardy : Un Long Chant d'amour*, p.11.
3. Locoge, Benjamin, 'Françoise Hardy: Mes chansons m'aidaient à supporter mes douleurs ('My Songs Helped me to Endure My Pains'), *Paris Match*, 23 March 2021.

33
Living Alone: Solitude

In 2010, Françoise was interviewed on Swiss television. This followed the launch of her new album *La Pluie sans parapluie* ('Rain Without an Umbrella'). What did the eponymous song, which was track 4 of the album, mean to her, she was asked?

Françoise: 'I did not write this song, but it represents a picture of a lack of protection and, of course, loneliness.'

Interviewer: 'You have been singing for about 50 years and the solitude is always here with you. Is it your companion?'

Whereupon Françoise distinguished between 'two types of solitude', compulsory, and voluntary. There is 'the solitude you put up with and which is very hard to live with and can be painful', and there is 'the solitude you choose to live with'. Now that she was 'getting older', she had decided to choose a life of solitude. This was 'necessary for me', she said, in order to 'help me to recover'. And having made the choice, 'I feel free. I can do whatever I like'.

Referring to, *Tous les Garçons et les Filles*, the interviewer remarked, 'You were 18 years old when you became famous by singing this song. What do you think when you look back at yourself in that time?'

Françoise: 'I do not need to look back to know how I am. I am still the same. I have always been shy, very sentimental, and most of the time uncomfortable in life.'

The song *Tous les Garçons et les Filles,* she said, was 'the realization of fantasies, and the person who sings that song made the promise not to blame the other with her personal needs'. The allusion is clearly to Jacques Dutronc, and that she would not blame him for the fact that she was 'needy'.

Interviewer: 'Anguish has always been part of your life?'

Françoise: 'It is more like anxiety. When you are not very well physically, and you feel down, or you have no news from somebody you like. But it could become anguish at some point'. This was probably a reference to her and Jacques's beloved son Thomas Dutronc, who had a busy life of travel to fulfil his obligations as a musician.[1]

This interview was revealing, if not shocking. Françoise confessed that she had felt lonely, unprotected, uncomfortable, and anxious for all of her adult life. However, she had decided to internalise her anguish and her 'words of love', and to keep to herself and to be alone.

In 2011, said Quinonero, for health reasons Françoise relocated to a three-room bungalow with garden near the parc de Bagatelle, in the 16th arrondissement. 'From then on, she lived alone. There was no more space for Jacques Dutronc, exiled in Corsica. "He feels homeless" she joked.'[2] Françoise's sole ambition now was to 'remain peaceful and relatively at ease in [her] little bunker'.[3]

What was left for Françoise, given the situation? Was there anything positive in her life, to ameliorate the situation? Yes, the joy she felt in the fact that Thomas was happy and making a success of his musical career.

---

1. Françoise Hardy, 'Ma Solitude est un choix' ('My Loneliness is A Choice'), interview for Swiss television, 2010, YouTube.
2. *Le Monde*, 7 November 2012, in Quinonero, Frédéric, *Françoise Hardy : Un Long Chant d'amour*, p.331.
3. Hardy, Françoise, Interview with the author (Quinonero), in Quinonero, Frédéric, *Françoise Hardy : Un Long Chant d'amour*, p.337.

34
A 'Thank You' to Jacques!

Astonishing as it may seem, despite all, Françoise felt no bitterness towards Jacques. In fact, she expressed her gratitude to him: 'The feelings you can have for someone you have known for this long, who gets old at the same time as you, are very mixed. There is a whole range of sentiments and emotions. You do not forget the intense moments of a love story and you want to thank that person for having spiced up your life in this way.'[1]

---

1. *La Presse*, Quebec, 21 November 2012, in Quinonero, Frédéric, *Françoise Hardy : Un Long Chant d'amour*, pp.337-8.

35
Some Help and Guidance for the Avoider

Some, including Françoise, would argue that Jacques, for all his gung-ho attitude and his bravado, was a victim just as much as she was.

For the 'avoider', advice and guidance is available today which may not have been available during the early years of Jacques's acquaintance with Françoise. Though if it had been, whether he would have wished to avail himself of it is by no means certain.

Levine and Heller's advice was that an avoider such as Jacques should acknowledge his 'need for space – whether emotional or physical – when things get too close, and then learn how to communicate that need'. He must also make it clear to his partner (in this case Françoise), that this is not because of any problem with her, but it would apply to any relationship entered into by the avoider.[1]

What to do 'When you feel an irrepressible need to bolt'? The answer: 'Use effective communication to explain to your partner that you need some space and that you'd like to find a way of doing so that is acceptable to him or her'. And having done so, make sure 'that the other person's needs are taken care of'.[2]

Sadly, Jacques's requirement for 'space' left Françoise with a broken heart! A more promising way forward was suggested by Diana Boettcher. Said she: 'In order to treat and ultimately overcome fear of commitment, it is important that those affected first recognize and also acknowledge that they suffer from an anxiety disorder (but Jacques does not seem to have a problem with the way he is and with his life in general. Françoise is the one complaining). Once this step has been taken, psychotherapy or professional counselling makes sense in order to combat the fear of relationships. In this way, those affected can find out the cause of their fear and get to the bottom of the problem. After all, it is rarely possible to come to terms with traumatic experiences without help. However, this is an essential prerequisite for overcoming the anxiety disorder.'[3]

1. Levine, Amir, and Rachel S. F. Heller, *Attached*, pp.239-40.
2. Ibid, p.234.
3. Boettcher, Diana, 'Commitment Anxiety: The Fear of Closeness', Couples Therapy Berlin, 8 September 2018, online.

36
Some of Françoise's Other Admirers

Françoise made some insightful and often amusing comments about some of her other admirers.

Mick Jagger

Said Françoise, 'I met him on the street, and he smiled to me, and I smiled to him, and I thought I would never recover.' That was in London in July 1965. She laughed. 'He was like an angel, really. A dark angel.' She can't stop chuckling. 'He is the first one, he doesn't know that, who gave me a little more confidence in myself, because in an interview for a French magazine for young girls, he said that I was his ideal woman.'[1]

'In fact, from the moment I went to England, I had a little more confidence, because in France the image I had was the image of a shy girl.' However, she laughed, 'when I went to England, I had another image. I felt, for instance, that the journalists were much more interested in my look than in my song'.[2]

David Bowie

Bowie had declared that everyone was in love with Françoise. But, said she, 'It's impossible for me to believe it. I think he has said that because it was for French TV, that's all, and I think it's certainly very exaggerated'.[3]

Bob Dylan

In 1966, at a concert at the Paris Olympia, a concert venue in the 9th arrondissement, said Françoise, Dylan 'was in very bad shape. He was not very well singing, he was not very well playing the guitar, he was often out of tune, things like that. And the interval lasted a very long time. The audience began whistling. And suddenly somebody came to me, and said, "He will not go back to the stage if you do not go to his dressing room to meet him". So, I did!'

'I didn't speak very well English, and he wasn't speaking French, so it was really terrible. And he played to me two songs which were not released at the time: *Just Like a Woman,* and *I Want You.* [sic]'

In late August 1969 Françoise attended the Isle of Wight Festival, in which Bob Dylan was one of the stars.[4]

'A few years ago, I read in the press that he had asked about me.' She laughed uproariously. 'So, I was very flattered, really!'[5]

Brian Jones

Françoise, said Quinonero, had 'observed the dichotomy between the innocent and naive singing youth of De Gaulle's France [Charles de Gaulle, French President from 1959 to 1969], where she belonged, and the emancipated, sexually liberated youth taking shape in Britain where it was leading a pop and cultural avant-garde, ready to revolutionise the world. And so, she remembered a dinner invitation from Brian Jones, who had just got together with [German-Italian actress] Anita Pallenberg, a stunning top model who would become Keith Richards's girlfriend'. This was in 1965.[6]

Said Françoise, 'They were wondering if I had accepted their invitation because I was interested in him or in her'. This provoked laughter! 'My fiancé, Jean-Marie Périer, was away on a reporting trip, and some people thought that I was a lesbian'.[7]

1. 'Falling for Françoise', A Falling Tree Production for BBC Radio 4, 2011.
2. Ibid.
3. Ibid.

4. Hardy, Françoise, *The Despair of Monkeys and Other Trifles*, p.54.
5. 'Falling for Françoise', A Falling Tree Production for BBC Radio 4, 2011.
6. Quinonero, Frédéric, *Françoise Hardy : Un Long Chant d'amour*, p.109.
7. *The Independent*, 5 February 2005.

37
The Camera Never Lies!

Photograph and film of Françoise exist, dating from her childhood onwards. In her biography *The Despair of Monkeys and Other Trifles*, she included several photographs which clearly had a special significance for her. One person who does not appear in the 'picture gallery', however, is her sister Michèle, with whom she was never able to establish a happy relationship.

Her maternal grandmother Jeanne Hardy

Françoise described Jeanne Hardy as her 'despicable grandmother', and she is included, presumably, only because she appears here with her three daughters, Marie-Louise, Madeleine (Françoise's mother), who is sitting on her lap, and Suzanne.

Her mother Madeleine Jeanne Hardy

Madeleine had 'extremely blue eyes', said Françoise, and Pierre Dillard (Françoise's father) was 'madly in love with her'.

Her father Pierre Marie Étienne Dillard

Pierre is sitting outdoors in the sunshine, lovingly cradling the toddler Françoise in his arms.

Frau Wesler – 'Aunt Heidi'

A happy and smiling Françoise is sitting outdoors on a bench, between her mother Madeleine and her beloved 'Aunt Heidi' (Hedwig Wesler, a friend of the family), with Heidi's daughter Gertrud and son Gunni standing behind them. Françoise spent several idyllic summer holidays with the Wesler family in the 1950s.

Jean-Marie Périer

Here is Françoise at the Paris Olympia, with her arm around Jean-Marie Périer.

Françoise the film star

Here is Françoise in a bikini, by a swimming pool in Monte Carlo during the filming of *Grand Prix,* in 1966. She is slender and moderately curvaceous, giving the lie, once and for all, to her belief that she had an androgynous figure!

Mick Jagger

Here, Françoise, with a delighted smile on her face, and Jean-Marie Périer are meeting Mick Jagger at London's Olympia. She described Mick as 'bewitching'!

Tuca

Here are Françoise and her beloved friend, the Brazilian musician Tuca, outside the CBE Studios in Paris.

Salvador Dalí

Françoise has included no less than 5 photographs of herself and Dalí. In four of them she is looking at him attentively, and in the fifth, he has undoubtedly said something which made her laugh.

Bob Dylan

Backstage at London's Olympia in 1966, we see Bob Dylan and Françoise sitting on a wooden crate together. They are looking intently at one another, he attired in pyjama-style striped suit and sunglasses, with cigarette in hand, and she somewhat bemused.

Françoise's quizzical caption for this photograph is, 'What could we have had to say to each other?'

Françoise, Jacques, and baby Thomas

Three photographs are included of the trio. In one, Françoise is smiling broadly; in another, Jacques is holding up a furry toy rabbit, with a look of sheer delight on his face, but unfortunately Thomas is looking the other way.

Françoise and Jacques

A photograph of Françoise and Jacques at Monticello in Upper Corsica, in 1973. He has his arm around her and is looking at her lovingly; she is cupping his chin in her fingers. Another photograph taken in the mountains shows Jacques gazing at her affectionately with an arm around her shoulder, as she looks as demure as ever but avoids his gaze.

Jacques and Thomas

Here we have Jacques cuddling the toddler, Thomas. This, said Françoise, was her 'favourite photo of Thomas and his father'. It was taken in Corsica.

Françoise the model

Here is Françoise, modelling a highly impractical metallic dress designed by the Spanish fashion designer Paco Rabanne. When it went out of shape, it had to be adjusted with pliers! It weighed 9 kilograms!

The wedding

Here are Jacques and Françoise on their wedding day, 30 March 1981, at the Town Hall, Monticello, in Upper Corsica. Françoise sits impassively with arms folded in a defensive position as Jacques puffs on his cigar. Both are casually dressed.

Thomas

Françoise chose to include this photograph of her son Thomas as a young man, she said, 'because his expression makes me melt'.

Film and photographs from other sources

Many other images of Françoise exist (quite apart from those that she chose to include in her autobiography) and also videos of her singing her various songs, which are available on YouTube. For example, looking somewhat incongruous wearing the helmet of a Formula One racing driver, taken during the filming of *Grand Prix*; sitting at the wheel of a racing car, her hair cropped uncharacteristically short; sitting astride an enormous stationary motorcycle, as she is obliged to point her toes in order to touch the ground, despite her long legs!

Françoise had the perfect figure for a model of her era, tall, slender, and wide in the shoulder. On the rare occasions that she did not look stylish, this was the fault of the fashion house designer, not herself. Furthermore, she was always graceful in her movements. Therefore, only very rarely is a photograph or film of Françoise unflattering as, for instance, when she is pictured strolling through a park, incongruously dressed in what appears to be a trouser suit made of aluminium foil! Not surprisingly, this fails to arouse the attention of an elderly gentleman who is snoozing on an adjacent park bench!

And here is Françoise, standing in front of the Eiffel Tower, her arm outstretched and holding a red rose, with the French tricolour in the other hand.

Many photographs were taken of Françoise against a backdrop of woods and trees, communing with nature being one of her favourite pastimes. Here, with a tree in the background, she is looking particularly demure, with black Alice band and russet coloured dress with black and white motif.

Here she is, smiling broadly for once as she points to the television set where she herself is appearing.

Another photograph shows Françoise gazing up adoringly at a bust of the French poet, writer, and art critic of Polish-Belarusian descent, Guillaume Apollinaire. In his poem, *Zone*, Apollinaire describes how a love that he once had was more of an 'affliction' than a blessing, and that for a long period he had 'lived like a fool' and wasted his opportunities. Such themes as these, together with the passage of time and wasted time would surely have resonated with Françoise!

Here she is, sitting on a highly decorated throne-like chair – which some might say was highly appropriate! In one hand she holds her guitar, in the other is the French flag ('Tricolour'), and at her feet is an enormous Afghan hound.

In a delightful scene, a youthful Françoise is standing in the middle of a quiet road being filmed by a young photographer who is on one knee! With her are two lady friends, and all are smiling.

Here we have Françoise and Jacques sitting beside a swimming pool. She is looking on benignly as he plays his guitar

Next, Françoise is sitting in a park reading a book – one of her favourite pastimes -, while an unidentified gentleman walks behind her dressed in a smart suit, never imagining for a moment that one day his photograph would be seen all over the world!

Françoise is seen in various situations; relaxing as she strolls along with a female friend, as they each enjoy an ice cream; sitting in a speeding motorboat with another female friend.

More images of Françoise are to be seen in a French documentary by Matthieu Jaubert and Émilie Valentin entitled *Françoise Hardy la discrète*. Following the birth of their baby, Thomas, here is Jacques, looking at her tenderly and stroking her cheek with two fingers of his left hand. Both have expressions of absolute joy on their faces. And here is Françoise returning the favour by kissing Jacques, as he puts his arm around her.

Finally, here is Françoise, doing what she loved best, singing to herself whilst strumming her guitar and writing down the music that she is composing.[1]

What conclusions, if any, can be drawn from a perusal of such film and photographs? What is noticeable is the contrast between the joyful looking Françoise of her youth, and the serious looking Françoise of her adulthood. It is visible that in early photographs and film, Françoise smiles readily, and is animated and demonstrative. But in her adult life, the former impression of uninhibited joie de vivre has virtually vanished, although occasionally, the ghost of a smile plays around her lips.

Admittedly, 'grown ups' tend to be less boisterous and playful than youngsters, but the adult Françoise often displays something of a haunted look. All too often, she appears to be in a kind of melancholic trance. Was she trained always to look serious, perhaps by those who promoted her and her music? Or was there something troubling her; i.e the corrosive effect of her deteriorating relationship with Jacques?

Perhaps the saddest and most soulful image of Françoise is the one which appears on the jacket cover of her autobiography *Françoise Hardy: The Despair of Monkeys and Other Trifles* (*Le Désespoir des singes et autres bagatelles)*. Her expressionless face and lifeless eyes surely reflect her feelings, as indicated by the title of her book, those of despair.

Millions throughout the world loved and admired Françoise, and still do, and they sense her vulnerability and feel protective towards her. In short, they are concerned for her welfare, even though the vast majority of them would never meet her. And for them, the manner in which she acknowledged her despair in an open and honest manner is another endearing attraction.

1. Matthieu Jaubert, Émilie Valentin, *Françoise Hardy la discrète*, Arte France, Ex Nihilo Zergen, 2021.

38
Sylvie Duval

When Jacques called Françoise from Corsica and told her that he was happy, she declared, 'I had never heard him say that before, even when he was with me. Of course, there have been times when I knew he was well, but it was unusual to hear him utter the word "happy". He went on to explain that he had met someone. I was delighted for him as, in view of the mid-life crisis, I had been feeling detached for a while'.[1]

When Françoise learned that the object of Jacques's affections was Sylvie Duval, she declared, 'In any relationship that has been ongoing for thirty years, there are inevitably crises, other people. Do you overcome them? Do you decide to give in the first time you get stabbed? Do you find a new *modus vivendi*?'[2]

Françoise's patience seemed inexhaustible. However, even she had her limitations. 'Becoming your husband's best friend, I find that beautiful. It is not as though everything is always fantastic, far from it. I regularly want to kill him, and the feeling is undoubtedly mutual.'[3]

1. *La Libre Belgique*, 24 October 2008, in Quinonero, Frédéric, *Françoise Hardy : Un Long Chant d'amour*, p.303.
2. *Paris Match*, No. 2649, 2 March 2000, in Quinonero, Frédéric, *Françoise Hardy : Un Long Chant d'amour*, p.303.
3. Leydier, Michel, *Jacques Dutronc, La Bio*, in Quinonero, Frédéric, *Françoise Hardy : Un Long Chant d'amour*, p.304.

39
The Significance of Eye Contact

A striking feature of the photographs and film footage that exist from the time that Françoise first met Jacques Dutronc is that, whereas he evidently had no problem in looking at her directly, she for her part rarely makes eye contact with him. And was it not French poet Guillaume de Salluste du Bartas (1544-1590) who described the eyes as 'These windows to the soul'?

Said US writers and publishers Brett and Kate McKay: 'Not only does increased eye contact make you seem more appealing in pretty much every way to those you interact with, it also improves the quality of that interaction. Eye contact imparts a sense of intimacy to your exchanges and leaves the receiver of your gaze feeling more positive about your interaction and connected to you. In short, making greater eye contact with others can increase the quality of all of your face-to-face interactions; there is no area of your life where being seen as more attractive, confident, and trustworthy wouldn't be a boon.'

Françoise was both attractive and trustworthy, and she *comes across* as being confident, at least outwardly, even if a little shy, although she did admit to having 'nerves' prior to giving a musical performance. So why her failure to make eye contact with Jacques?

Continued Brett and Kate McKay: 'That we give so much credence to the idea that we can read someone from what's in their eyes is due to the fact that, even when we hide what we're really thinking and feeling in our body language and facial expressions, it's often still revealed in our eyes. "The eyes don't lie" as people say. This is why poker players often wear sunglasses in order to disguise their reactions to the hands they're dealt.'

If it was the case that Françoise's eye avoidance was because she was determined to hide her innermost thoughts from Jacques, what were these thoughts that she was trying to hide from him, and why? This is a matter of conjecture. However, to make an educated guess:

'One of the most common reasons that people avoid eye contact is from simple insecurity.' By her own admission, Françoise longed for a loving and companionable relationship, and all the more so as her relationship with her mother Madeleine, upon whom she had relied all of her life, had gradually deteriorated. This is not to say that Jacques was not loving towards her, but to have a lover who was here one minute and gone the next was perhaps even worse than having nobody at all, in the sense that every time Jacques left her, this stoked up all Françoise's feelings of insecurity. In short, she would have felt bereft.

'Eye contact invites more interaction, and you might not want people to take a closer look at you [i.e. yourself] because of how you feel about yourself. This lack of confidence can be rooted in insecurity over one's physical appearance, or the state of one's mind.'

Astonishing as it may seem, Françoise, by her own admission, had a negative and self-critical opinion about her physical appearance, and as far as her relationship with Jacques was concerned, she was far from confident, even after they were married.

It is also the case, concluded Brett and Kate McKay, 'that people who suffer from depression — which can do a number [i.e. have a negative effect] on a person's self-confidence – are less likely to make eye contact with people'. Was Françoise depressed? Anyone who has read her biography will come to the inevitable conclusion that yes, she was, as the inclusion of the word 'despair' in the title of her autobiography indicates.[1]

Since her younger days, when her grandmother Jeanne denigrated her, Françoise had experienced feelings of shame and of rejection: 'From as long as I recall, I have suffered from having to deal with people who did not love me, whom I did not love, people I did not feel connected to but whom I had to put up with and to love because they were family! I think my mother was the only one I loved when I was a child. I loved no one else.'[2]

No wonder Françoise longed for a loving relationship that offered closeness, togetherness, and companionship, and although

Jacques undoubtedly loved her, the tragedy of Françoise's life was that such sentiments were anathemas to him.

1. 'Look 'Em in the Eye: Part 1 – The Importance of Eye Contact', The Art of Manliness, 25 February 2021, online.
2. Massenet, Ariane et Beatrice, *Mères et Fils : Ce que je voudrais te dire*, Aubanel, 2008.

40
'Falling for Françoise'

In 2011, Françoise gave a revealing interview to one of her English admirers, broadcaster, and journalist John Andrew. This formed the basis for 'Falling for Françoise', a programme aired on BBC Radio 4. Other participants were fellow Hardy enthusiasts Tony Bray, journalist Laura Barton, and Warren Gilbert.

Andrew had first visited France as a schoolboy in the 1960s, when he was in the 6th form. Said he, 'I fell in love with the voice of a certain young singer, and I wasn't alone. Just about every teenage boy who had heard or seen Françoise Hardy was equally smitten'.

Tony Bray stated that 'when Françoise came along, singing fantastic songs, a beautiful, intelligent girl, she was on a completely different planet from the rest of the artists who were around at that time'. And Laura Barton said of Françoise, 'I love the dusky sweetness of her voice'. Her songs, she said, had a 'dream like' quality. Furthermore, 'They don't live entirely in that era. They still sound contemporary'.

Warren Gilbert declared that it was his intention to collect every recording that Françoise had ever made, but this proved to be an impossible task. She was a workaholic, and her *Discographie* (descriptive catalogue of musical recordings) runs to no less than 63 pages![1]

In 2011, John returned to France, and met Françoise in person at the headquarter of EMI Music France in Montmartre, where she insisted on having an interpreter present. This, presumably, was because she did not wish to be misquoted.

Françoise began on a humorous note. 'At the very moment I was born there was an alert [air-raid warning]'. This, she said with a chuckle, might have had 'something to do with the fact that I am a very anxious person. I have always been'. FF

In regard to *Tous les Garçons et les Filles*, she had mixed feelings. This 'was my most famous song, even today, and I never had since this first song such a success, and it is not my best song. Far from it'.[2]

Following the success of her song *Dans le monde entier*, said Françoise, she was engaged by the London's Savoy Hotel. 'After the show I went to a discotheque to have something to eat where, sometimes, I met the famous singers of the time, especially Brian Jones and Mick Jagger. But I was very shy in my corner saying nothing, and I saw them passing by. I was like a very shy fan, you know', she said with a chuckle.[3]

How did Françoise cope with fame? 'At the same time, I met my first boyfriend, Jean-Marie Périer, and I was only preoccupied by my personal life, and by him, and by the songs which inspired me. And the rest, I didn't see it. I didn't care. I didn't enjoy it at all; everything that happens when all of a sudden you become very famous. It's very difficult for me, quite impossible, to stand to be admired too much, you know. It's not a normal situation. No, I don't like that at all.'[4]

When she was adopted by various fashion houses, said Françoise, it was 'a trauma. At the time, it was work. Things I had to do. A chore. I didn't enjoy it at all'.[5]

Said British singer-songwriter Ben Christophers about Françoise: 'She's got such grace, and carries it with some kind of humble silence'.[6]

Of Iggy Pop, Françoise declared him to be 'the nicest "bad boy" I've ever met, and it was a great moment, really. I was very nervous because Iggy Pop is a very good singer. He let me [have] the choice of the song. "Don't choose a too jazzy song because [she lowers her voice] I'm not too good at it", he says to me on the phone', and she laughed![7]

'It's always very difficult to be happy with everything', said Françoise. However, British singer-songwriter Ben Christophers' song *My Beautiful Demon*, which she sang as a duet with him

(2006), and *I'll Be Seeing You* (1997) which she sang as a duet with Iggy Pop, 'are two of my favourite recordings. It's almost perfect'.[8]

Referring to the world of show business, said Françoise 'What is difficult with this activity is, it's a bubble, and it's also in my temperament to remain closed in'. But being isolated in this way, she said, was 'not a healthy thing'.[9]

'Maybe it's difficult for people to understand, said Françoise, 'but I've always lived for my personal life. I'm not comfortable with my professional life, really. So, the word "icon", it's as though you were talking about somebody else, you know. It's not me, really.'[10] Modesty is one of Françoise's trademarks.

The success that she had, said Françoise, 'never made me confident with myself and with my work. I feel happy and secure when I am on my bed in my room with a good book'.[11]

1. Quinonero, Frédéric, *Françoise Hardy : Un Long Chant d'amour*, pp.343-406.
2. 'Falling for Françoise', A Falling Tree Production for BBC Radio 4, 2011.
3. Ibid.
4. Ibid.
5. Ibid.
6. Ibid.
7. Ibid.
8. Ibid.
9. Ibid.
10. Ibid.
11. Ibid.

41
Illness

On 1 January 2005 Françoise learned that she was suffering from lymphoma (cancer of the lymphatic system). 'Never was I so anxious, but the worst was to realize the disarray of those close to me, particularly my son'.[1] This was a clear allusion to the fact that Thomas was already mourning the very recent death of his paternal grandfather. Typically, Françoise, despite her own plight, was thinking of others.

In that year of 2005, Françoise was awarded France's Victoires de la Musique - Female Artist of the Year - in recognition of her outstanding achievement in the music industry. This was for her album *Tant de belles choses* ('All the Beautiful Things'). At the age of 74, her 24th studio album, *Personne d'autre* was released (in April 2018).

1. *Fusées*, No. 9, October 2005, in Quinonero, Frédéric, *Françoise Hardy : Un Long Chant d'amour*, p.316.

42
Faith; Mortality; The Afterlife

In regard to religion, said Françoise in 2005, 'I had some beliefs, but I did not grasp them sufficiently to be totally serene'. Furthermore, 'The help derived from one's belief in the afterlife, as strong as it may be, does unfortunately prevent neither physical suffering nor decay'.[1]

In 2010 Françoise declared: 'As a teenager, when I discovered the narrow moralistic approach of the Judeo-Christian doctrine, I moved away from religion', said Françoise. 'However, it wasn't long before I realized how thin the line is between a rigid moralistic approach and an absence of morality, or lack of ethics, which I find so alienating. It is difficult to find the right balance between these two extremes. In short, I typically abandoned the religion of my youth, whilst continuing to be attracted by mystics and spiritual scriptures.'[2]

Of her song *Tant de belles choses* Françoise declared, 'I tried to pour into it all the love I feel for those close to me, particularly my son, as well as the belief garnered from spiritual texts I have read, that death is a matter for the body, not for the spirit, so that strong terrestrial links remain in other ways, whatever happens'.[3]

Françoise believed in an 'afterlife', and in the possibility of reincarnation. 'If that is how it is, if this theory of reincarnation stands, I tell myself that, knowing what I now know, if ever I were to reincarnate and have another relationship with someone who meant a lot to me, I hope that we would do a lot better. This was a first draft and next time we will write it out properly.'[4]

She looked forward to meeting up again with Jacques, whom she referred to as her 'future widower', somewhere else, 'in another life' ('dans une autre vie'), 'to love more and better than today' ('pour aimer plus et mieux qu'aujourdhui').

1. *Platine*, No. 118, February 2005, in Quinonero, Frédéric, *Françoise Hardy : Un Long Chant d'amour*, p.318.
2. *Clés*, October-November 2010, in Quinonero, Frédéric, *Françoise Hardy : Un Long Chant d'amour*, p.30.
3. *Fusées*, No. 9, October 2005, in Quinonero, Frédéric, *Françoise Hardy : Un Long Chant d'amour*, p.316.
4. *L'Invite*, TV5 Monde, 8 February 2013, in Quinonero, Frédéric, *Françoise Hardy : Un Long Chant d'amour*, p.338.

Epilogue

Jacques Dutronc seldom spoke about his feelings for Françoise, apart from on one occasion, on 19 June 2021, when he was interviewed by French journalist and TV host Michel Denisot for Europe 1 radio.

About Françoise, he said, 'The more things progressed, the more she gave me caviar [this word being the same in both French and English]'. However, he immediately realized that he had made a 'slip of the tongue'. What he meant to have said was, 'the more she gave me "cafard"', which in French has two meanings, either 'the blues' (which is probably what he intended), or 'a cockroach' (which doesn't make sense).

Jacques corrected himself. 'She gave me the blues', he said, and then joked, 'the caviar came later, because she sold tons of records [meaning that she could afford to buy him caviar because she was then making plenty of money]' Finally, said Jacques, 'La SACEM [organisation responsible for paying royalties to authors and composers], here I came!'[1]

When Jacques stated that Françoise gave him 'the blues' – a feeling of melancholy, sadness, or depression, ODE- was this said in jest, or did he mean it? And if he meant it, Françoise, who was undoubtedly aware of his comment, would have been horrified. Or was she past caring by that stage? Who knows? Nonetheless Jacques enjoyed the prospect of the wealth that Françoise generated, which was not unreasonable, given that some of their song compositions and productions were joint enterprises. But of course, he was wealthy in his own right.

As for Françoise, did she ever entirely let herself go, and speak frankly and uninhibitedly about her feelings for Jacques, and what she perceived as his feelings for her? The answer is to be found in her novel *L'Amour fou*, (published 2012).

In Françoise's novel *L'Amour fou*, published in 2012, there are similarities between the lives of the two principal characters and the lives of Francoise and Jacques. This is too much of a coincidence. In fact, so great are these similarities that it is obvious that in writing the book, Françoise was reliving her life vicariously, through the female, who is not named. The male character is referred to as 'X'. Furthermore, by giving the novel the title of the novel, 'Mad', or 'Insane Love', the author is implying that what she is describing is not a rational love affair.

In the following narrative, where the quotations are from *L'Amour fou*, 'She' and 'X' will be taken to be synonymous with Françoise and Jacques.

For Françoise, hope springs eternal:

'In spite of her defeatism, she first waited for a sign which would give her a clue as to what X was feeling for her (a mere hint of friendliness would have done), but he was extraordinarily inexpressive and impersonal.'[2]

Françoise wonders whether Jacques is autistic

'Something suggested that X had autistic tendencies, and it crossed her mind that maybe he was better equipped to be loved than to love.'[3]

Autism is defined as 'a mental condition, present from early childhood, characterized by great difficulty in communicating and forming relationships with other people and in using language and abstract concepts'.[4] This certainly does not apply to Jacques.

Jacques himself might have suggested that Françoise was obsessional in respect of her love for him, to obsess being defined as 'to preoccupy or fill the mind of someone continually and to a troubling extent; to be constantly talking or worrying about something [i.e. Jacques]'.[5]

'Obsessive Love Disorder' is not classified as a psychiatric disorder. Nevertheless, it can impact severely on a relationship. Said US psychiatrist Amelia Alvin, 'In obsessive love disorder, people take their protective nature to lengths and start controlling the person they love'.[6]

Symptoms of this disorder can include: 'possessive thoughts*; low self-esteem*; a need for constant contact such as repeated phone calls and messages*; feelings of intense jealousy; a sense of disbelief in the relationship*; spying; extreme emotional displays; hyper-sensitivity; ignoring loved ones' personal boundaries; seeking constant validation*.'[7]

Some, if not all of these characteristics, in particular those marked with an asterisk, may certainly be applied to Françoise, and she herself would probably not deny it.

Was Françoise displaying the signs of erotomania, defined as 'a delusion in which a person (typically a woman) believes that another person (typically of higher social status) is in love with them'?[8] Evidently not, because her chief anxiety was that Jacques was not in love with her, and she desperately looked for signs to prove herself wrong.

For Françoise, the agony of a one-sided love

'The violence of the love he inspired in her, exacerbated by the utter belief this love was impossible, brought tears to her eyes and she walked away.'[9]

Doubts creep in. Has she got the wrong idea about Jacques, Françoise asks herself?

'Part of her … kept warning her that she may be mistaken, that what she imagined from the way things appeared had certainly more to do with her own reality than his.'[10]

Françoise has sufficient insight to entertain the possibility that her belief that Jacques loved her was a construct, a figment of her imagination. The result for her: shock, and indescribable sadness.

<u>When Jacques did reach out to Françoise, was this simply a cry for help, because he felt vulnerable?</u>

'On the rare occasions that he smiled at her, there was a contrast between his usual coldness and the striking impression he suddenly gave of being totally disarmed, of offering himself totally. She wondered if this contrast was indicative of a vulnerability which he often tried to fight off by hiding behind his bulletproof mask, or if, against all expectations, he trusted her specifically, whether consciously or not.'[11]

<u>Was it true, that Jacques *did* occasionally reciprocate Françoise's feelings, or did she imagine it?</u>

'Sometimes … she thought she could feel a reciprocity which enthused her but, very quickly, the fear that it was just wishful thinking forced her to crash back down to a dark and shaky earth, riddled with doubt.'[12]

<u>Jacques 'turns Françoise on' like no other man</u>

'X was the first person whose vibes she thought she could physically feel.'[13]

<u>Was Jacques passionate towards other women, even though he was not passionate towards Françoise? If so, she would find this unbearable.</u>

'The anticipation of this woman, who would sooner or later appear on the scene, and who she could never be herself, hurt her beyond belief. She imagined her with everything she had never had and would never have: him, him above all.'[14]

    These are perhaps the most poignant and heartrending words that Françoise ever wrote!

Paradoxically, it is Jacques's character defects that Françoise finds so alluring, such as:

'Some rather worrying character traits: passivity, complacency, letting oneself go… She forgot that these were the very defects which, far from being off putting, inflame the heart of the one who has been harpooned by love.'[15]

Whereas Françoise longs for and lives for the times when she and Jacques can be together, he remains silent.

'Her rare exchanges with X had become so necessary for her that knowing she would be deprived of them terrified her. Nothing in his behaviour could indicate that he felt the same way. When the day arrived, she walked up to the table where he was eating with others and informed him that she was leaving. Seeming slightly surprised, he got up and awkwardly shook the hand she was holding out. One last smile and it was over.'[16]

Françoise believes that she is attracted to Jacques because he has qualities that she lacks, and because of this she regards herself as 'unlovable'.

'Too often she had had the paralysing sensation of being attracted by what she was lacking: charm, ambiguity, mystery. Yet, she at times imagined that someone may see some qualities in her, but the knowledge of this possibility did nothing to lessen the discomfort brought on by her self-deprecating ways.'[17]

The penny finally drops, as Françoise realizes the absurdity and futility of hoping and dreaming as far as a meaningful relationship with Jacques was concerned.

'You … endeavoured to complain about the rigidity of the feelings which made me hang on so stubbornly and ridiculously to my teenagers' dreams and to the "basic mix" that was our relationship. You then rejected my request for you to come and sit next to me, using as a compelling excuse the fact that you could not see the point in answering this kind of need unless it was shared. How you could talk about a basic mix, I whispered, when the shortest of moments spent with the one you love is so priceless? Such moments are worth nothing if they are not reciprocated, he answered back. I suggested that love needs presence and exchange more than a reciprocity which is always imaginary. But you were obviously annoyed by the turn things were taking and cut me short, accusing me bluntly of not being able to distinguish between love and decay.'[18]

The use of the words 'love' and 'decay' suggests that yes, Jacques had once loved her, but that this love had withered on the proverbial vine.

Finally:

'Everything had been said. I had to get up, go, get back to a life more deadly than death itself. I stumbled towards the door, and you let me walk out of your life with what I perceived to be a mix of indifference and relief.'[19]

Said French classical music journalist Olivier Bellamy, 'It is when she laughs that I truly recognise Françoise. She has the appearance of someone very melancholic, her melancholy is part of us; it is a very personal melancholy which resonates with us in the way she expresses it'.[20]

Françoise's plaintive songs, written over more than five decades, in which she expressed her deepest feelings for Jacques, may be regarded collectively as one of the longest love letters in history. Sadly, it remained largely unanswered.

In respect of Jacques, said Françoise, 'In spite of all the difficulties inherent to being in love, the years I spent with him, from 1974 to 1988, are the best of my life. This is partially down to him, but also down to our son, Thomas'.[21]

Finally, in the 'Acknowledgments' section of her book, *Françoise Hardy: Un long chant d'amour* (published 2017) Françoise includes the words 'Merci à ma famille' – 'Thank you to my family; and also, most poignantly, 'À mon père' – 'To my father'.

Today, thanks to the wonders of modern technology, Françoise can be resurrected at any moment of her singing career, at the simple press of a button on the television's remote control. And there she is, the epitome of French elegance and style!

(Albin Michel, Paris, 2012)

1. Jacques Dutronc, interviewed by French journalist and TV host Michel Denisot for Europe 1, 19 June 2021.
2. Hardy, Françoise, *L'Amour fou*, p.11.
3. Ibid, p.11.
4. Soanes, Catherine and Angus Stevenson (Editors), *Oxford Dictionary of English*.
5. Ibid.
6. Alvin, Amelia, Mango Clinic, Florida.
7. Hope Gillette, 'All About Obsessive Love Disorder', PsychCentral, 9 August 2021.
8. Soanes, Catherine and Angus Stevenson (Editors), *Oxford Dictionary of English*, op. cit.
9. Hardy, Françoise, *L'Amour fou*, op. cit., p.12.
10. Ibid, pp.12-13.
11. Ibid, p.13.
12. Ibid, p.14.
13. Ibid, p.14.
14. Ibid, p.15.
15. Ibid, p.15.
16. Ibid, pp.15-16.
17. Ibid, p.16.
18. Ibid, pp.146-7.
19. Ibid, p.147.
20. Marc-Olivier Fogiel, *Le Divan*, in Quinonero, Frédéric, *Françoise Hardy : Un Long Chant d'amour*, pp.313-4.
21. *Le Parisien*, 9 October 2008, in Quinonero, Frédéric, *Françoise Hardy : Un Long Chant d'amour*, p.251.

Biography

Bowlby, John, *Child Care and the Growth of Love* (Penguin Books, London, 1965)
Domain, Valérie, *Femmes de, Filles de : Portraits de femmes d'influence* (*First Editions*, Paris, 2005)
Hardy, Françoise, *L'Amour fou* (Albin Michel, Paris, 2012)
Hardy, Françoise, *Chansons sur toi et nous* (Équateurs, Paris, 2021)
Hardy, Françoise, *The Despair of Monkeys and Other Trifles* (Feral House, Port Townsend, Washington, USA, 2018)
Leydier, Michel, *Jacques Dutronc* (EJL, Paris, 1999)
Levine, Amir, and Rachel S. F. Heller, *Attached* (Bluebird, London, 2019)
Massenet, Ariane et Béatrice, *Mères et Fils : Ce que je voudrais te dire* (Aubanel, Dublin, Ireland, 2008)
Quinonero, Frédéric, *Françoise Hardy : Un Long Chant d'amour* (L'Archipel, Paris, 2017)
Soanes, Catherine and Angus Stevenson (Editors), *Oxford Dictionary of English* (Oxford University Press, Oxford, New York, 2005)
Stevenson, A., and Waite, M., *Concise Oxford English Dictionary*, (Oxford and New York, Oxford University Press, 2011)
Nouvelles Clés.
Le Nouvel Observateur.
L'Express.
Libération.
Les Essentiels.
Le Journal du Dimanche.
Salut les Copains.
Paris Match.

Index

Académie Française 34
Alesi, Hermès 39
Allemane, Benoît 81
Alvin, Amelia 152
Anka, Paul 28
Anthony, Richard 38
Apollinaire, Guillaume 138
À quoi ça sert? (Why even try?) 115
Astrologos 86
Aulnay-sous-Bois 14-15
Avedon, Richard 55
Averty, Jean-Christophe 54
Barnard, Christiaan 60
Bartas, Guillaume de Salluste du 141
Barton, Laura 144
Benarroch, Charles 'Charlot' 32, 41
Berger, Michel 61, 66, 85
Bernot, André 30
Blackwell, Charles 38
Boettcher, Diana 96-97, 129
Bowie, David 131
Bowlby, John 21-23
Brassens, Georges 62
Bray, Tony 144
Bruit de fond ('Background Noise') 117
Canal + French TV channel 86
Caulier, Cécile 39
Ce Soir ('This Evening') 118
Chansons sur toi et nous? ('Songs about You and Us?') 113
Château en Suède 39
Child Care and the Growth of Love 21
Christophers, Ben 145
Cléo (stage name of Joanna Klepko) 43
Cochran, Eddie 29
Comment te dire adieu? ('How To Say Goodbye To You?') 65

Comme tant d'autres ('Like So Many Others') 114
Courrèges, André 38
Dalai Lama 85
Dali, Salvador 56, 135
Daniel, Pascale 87
Dans le monde entier ('In the Whole World') 38, 145
Davis, Miles 34
Denisot, Michel 150
Dillard, Madeleine Jeanne (née Hardy) 11, 134
Dillard, Pierre Marie Étienne 11, 76, 134
Disques Vogue 30, 32-33, 39, 42-44, 53-54, 62-63
Donnez, Raymond 64
Dray, Daniel 41
Dumayet, Pierre 38
Dutronc, Jacques 41-44, 46-47, 52-54, 56-58, 60, 62-72, 78-80, 82-88, 90, 92-94, 96-99, 102-103, 106-109, 111-112, 115-118, 120-124, 126-129, 136, 138-143, 148, 150-155
Dutronc, Madeleine (née Sounier) 41, 69
Dutronc, Pierre 41
Dutronc, Thomas 68, 127
Duval, Sylvie 87, 140
Dylan, Bob 34, 131-132, 135
Éditions Alpha 43
Effeuille-moi le coeur ('Pull the Petals of my Heart') 50
EMI Music France 144
En résumé, en conclusion ('To Sum Up, to Conclude') 119
Estardy, Bernard 61
Et même ('And Even') 38
Europe No. 1 radio 33, 78, 150
Everly Brothers 28-29
Fain, Sammy 82
Filipacchi, Daniel 37
France-Soir 30
'Françoise Hardy Blues' 54
Françoise Hardy: The Despair of Monkeys and Other Trifles (*Le Désespoir des singes et autres bagatelles*) 13, 98, 134, 139
Frankenheimer, John 24, 51
Fury, Billy 29

Gainsbourg, Serge 81
Giannellia, Gilbert von 14, 19, 28
Gilbert, Warren 144
Glaser, Denise 38
Grand Prix 24, 44, 51, 55, 135, 137
Gray, Thomas 66
Guenet, Gilbert 33
Guétary, Georges 28-29
Hallyday, Johnny 33
Hardy, Claudius Alexandre 14, 21-22
Hardy, Louise Jeanne (née Milot) 14, 21-22
Hardy, Madeleine Jeanne (see Dillard)
Hardy, Michèle 11, 13-15, 19, 21, 76, 85, 87, 134
Hardy, Thomas 57
Hartuck, Mireille 32, 68, 85
Heller, Rachel S. F. 101, 109, 111
Houellebecq, Michel 86
ICP (Inter Chemicals and Plastics, Brussels, Belgium) 81
I'll be Seeing You 82, 146
Institut d'Études Politiques 29
Jagger, Mick 34, 131, 135, 145
J'ai fait de lui un rêve ('I Had a Dream about Him') 115
J'ai jeté mon coeur ('I Scattered my Heart) James, Henry 113
J'aurais voulu ('I Would Have Liked') 114
Je n'aime pas ce qu'il dit ('I Don't Like What He Is Saying') 118
Jones, Brian 132, 145
Kahal, Irving 82
Kalafate, Hadi 41, 44, 46, 54, 90-91
Lacome, Jacques 39
La Curée ('The Game is Over') 54
L'Amour fou, 75, 151
Lanzmann, Jacques 43, 54, 56, 90
La Pluie sans parapluie ('Rain Without Umbrella') 126
La Question ('The Question') 64, 117
Lara, Catherine 64
Le Cactus 56
Lee, Brenda 28-29
Lena 60, 62-64, 66

Les Pas ('The Steps') 121
Le Petit Prince 48
Le Temps d'amour ('The Time of Love') 43
Levine, Amir 101, 109, 111, 129
L'Important c'est d'aimer ('That Important Thing: Love') 69
L'Obscur Objet ('That Obscure Object') 120
Lubrano, Alain 81, 87
Madame Rose 32
McEnery, Peter 44, 54-55
McKay, Brett 141-142
McKay, Kate 141-142
McLaren, Malcolm 82
Même si ça fait mal ('Even If It Hurts') 81
Message personnel ('Personal Message') 66, 68
Mini-Mini-Mini 54
Mitchell, Eddy (stage name of Claude Moine] 43, 53
Modiano, Patrick 50
Mon Amie la rose, ('The Rose') 33, 39
Morisse, Lucien 43
Nicola, Jean-Pierre 68
Norman, Patrick (stage name of Yvon Éthier) 32
Oh! Oh! Chéri 33
Pagniez, Régis 37
Paris Match 33, 86
Partir quand même ('To Leave, No Matter What') 119
Pedersen, Guy 64
Périer, Jean-Marie 37-39, 55, 64, 66, 69, 75, 90, 132, 135, 145
Personne d'autre (No One Else) 122, 147
Petit Conservatoire de Mireille 32
Pivot, Bernard 34
Pompidou, Georges 56
Pop, Iggy 82, 145-146
Presley, Elvis 28, 30, 47, 63
Proust, Marcel 48
Quel dommage ('What a Shame') 122
Quinonero, Frédéric 33-34, 37, 39, 44, 46-48, 54-55, 58, 68, 111, 113, 127, 132
Rabanne, Paco 47, 136

Radio Luxembourg 27, 29
Radio Monte Carlo 81
Rendez-vous dans une autre vie ('Let's Meet in Another Life') 121
Revenge of the Flowers 81
Richard, Cliff 28-29
Roc, Lionel 60
Sabar, Jean-Pierre 60
Saint-Exupéry, Antoine de 48
Salvet, André 43
Samyn, Roger 33-34
Sanson, Véronique 66
Schneider, Romy 69, 107
Sedaka, Neil 29
Setti, Jean 33
Société des Auteurs, Compositeurs, et Éditeurs de Musique (SACEM) 33, 150
Soleil ('Sun') 65
Sonopresse 65
Sorbonne University 29-30, 76
Studio CBE, Paris 61
Tant de belles choses ('All the Beautiful Things')' 87, 147-148
The Rose 39
Ton Meilleur Ami ('Your Best Friend') 34
Tous les Garçons et les Filles ('All the Boys and Girls') 33-34, 57, 126, 145
Trammell, Bobby Lee 33
Trechikoff, Vladimir 60
Trois Petits Tours ('Three Little Turns') 123
Tu ressembles à tous ceux qui ont eu du chagrin ('You Resemble All Those Who Have Known Sorrow') 116
Tuca (given name Valeniza Zagni da Silva) 63-64, 135
Une balle au coeur 39
Vadim, Roger 55
Vartan, Sylvie 38
Vogue 56
Was mach' ich ohne dich? ('What would I do without you?') 51
Waters, Jessica 55

Wesler, Frau (see Wesler, Gertrud)
Wesler, Gertrud ('Aunt Heidi') 19, 134
Wesler, Gunni 19, 134
Wesler, Hedwig ('Aunt Heidi') 19, 134
Wolfsohn, Jacques 30, 39, 42-44, 47, 58, 62
Yared, Gabriel 75
Zouzou (stage name of Danièle Ciarlet 43, 90-91

About the Author

Andrew Norman was born in Newbury, Berkshire, UK in 1943. Having been educated at Thornhill High School, Gwelo, Southern Rhodesia (now Zimbabwe), Midsomer Norton Grammar School, and St Edmund Hall, Oxford, he qualified in medicine at the Radcliffe Infirmary. He has two children Bridget and Thomas, by his first wife.

From 1972-83, Andrew worked as a general practitioner in Poole, Dorset, before a spinal injury cut short his medical career. He is now an established writer whose published works include biographies of Charles Darwin, Winston Churchill, Thomas Hardy, T. E. Lawrence, Adolf Hitler, Agatha Christie, Enid Blyton, Beatrix Potter, Marilyn Monroe, and Sir Arthur Conan Doyle. Andrew married his second wife Rachel, in 2005.

Author's website: https://www.andrew-norman.co.uk
Amazon Profile: https://www.amazon.co.uk/-/e/BOOMCQL8JM

www.ingramcontent.com/pod-product-compliance
Lightning Source LLC
Chambersburg PA
CBHW072136160426
43197CB00012B/2133